DRAWING
with
PEN and INK

DRAWING
with
PEN and INK

ARTHUR L. GUPTILL
edited and revised by HENRY C. PITZ

 REINHOLD PUBLISHING CORPORATION • NEW YORK

©1961, Reinhold Publishing Corporation
    First Edition, 1928
All Rights Reserved
Printed in the United States of America
Library of Congress Catalog Card No. 61—10573

Designed by Henry C. Pitz
Printed by The Comet Press, Inc.
Bound by Publishers Book Bindery
Second Printing, Revised Edition, 1965

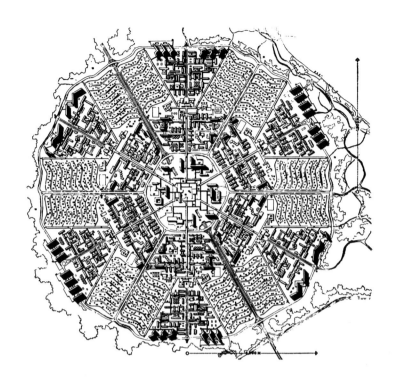

PREFACE

WHEN THE AUTHOR, in 1922, brought out, through the medium of THE PENCIL POINTS PRESS, INC., the volume *Sketching and Rendering in Pencil*, it met with a readier and a far more cordial reception than either he or the publishers had dared anticipate. Since its publication a gratifying number of letters concerning it have come from readers far and near. A great number have urged the publication of similar volumes dealing with other mediums of pictorial expression, and among these a large percentage have suggested a volume on drawing with pen and ink.

Inasmuch as there were already some excellent books devoted wholly to this subject, such as *Pen Drawing and Pen Draughtsmen* by Joseph Pennell, *Pen Drawing* by Charles D. Maginnis, *With Pen and Ink* by James Hall, *The Art of Pen Drawing* by G. M. Ellwood, and many others offering instruction in its rudiments or dealing with some special kinds of pen work, it at first seemed that there was no imperative need for an additional one.

It has been found on investigation, however, that some of these books are out of print or very expensive, so as time has gone on and more and more communications have come, asking for discussion of this or that phase of the subject, or urging the presentation of a new group of reproductions of pen work, it has been decided to comply, as far as possible, with these requests. This volume is the result.

Like its companion, *Sketching and Rendering in Pencil*, it is based partly on lectures and instruction given by the author in his classes in Art, Architecture, and Interior Decoration at Pratt Institute, Brooklyn, N. Y., over a period of some years, and partly on his experience as a professional illustrator. The material used at Pratt Institute has been thoroughly revised and greatly enlarged upon, so that this volume, as it now stands, offers, instead of definite courses of study planned for special groups of students, something of value to everyone who is interested in the art of pen drawing.

From the definite starting point of particularly comprehensive elementary chapters the reader is led naturally and easily, step by step, through chapters dealing with more advanced or complex phases of the subject, to final chapters treating special matters, some of which are of interest mainly to limited groups. In doing all this an attempt has been made to preserve the unity of each chapter, thus making the whole of greater value as a work of reference.

The illustrations for such a book are of particular importance. These which are here presented show many kinds of subjects, handled in a wide variety of ways. The elementary illustra- tions have been reproduced so far as possible at the exact or approximate size of the original drawings, so each individual pen stroke appears here much as it was drawn, both in size and character. Most of the illustrations by the author have been made, not mainly with the thought of beautifying the whole, but rather to meet the necessity of amplifying and clarifying the points brought out by the text. The supplementary illustrations, which speak for themselves as to quality and variety, have also been selected and arranged with this in mind, so that almost every drawing, aside from being an excellent example of pen work, done by an expert, fills some particular requirement here. The marginal sketches, in addition to serving as useful illustrations to the text, also function as a sort of pictorial index, as those on each page are related, when possible, to the text of the same or some nearby page.

Many and varied as our illustrations are, no effort has been made to include work by all the leading men. To do so in one volume would be almost impossible, and, in any case, contrary to our purpose. For we aim to offer practical instruction in the art of pen drawing rather than a statement of facts concerning its history or a discussion of the relative merits of the work of its followers. To those who wish to know more of its history and to see examples of the work of some of the leading pioneers in the art, we commend the above mentioned *Pen Drawing and Pen Draughtsmen* by Joseph Pennell.

—Arthur L. Guptill

EDITOR'S NOTE

Arthur L. Guptill's *Drawing With Pen and Ink* has been a landmark in the literature of ink technique for many years. The volume has gone through many printings and reached many thousands of students. It has been out of print for a number of years because the plates had become worn and a sharp reprint was no longer possible. A new edition would have entailed not only a complete new set of plates but the addition of new material. Fads, fashions and styles constantly affect the world of art and ink techniques have shown response to the times. Many ink drawings of today wear a different look from those of thirty years ago. A whole new company of artists has grown up with its own way of saying things.

In addition the cost of manufacturing has increased enormously during the last thirty years. A new book, the size of the original volume, would now have to be sold at a prohibitive price. So revision and condensation were necessities.

Thinking of my long friendship with Arthur L. Guptill and remembering the way he thought and wrote has helped, I trust, in my revision of his text. A number of chapters have been combined; several, covered in other books, have been dropped; two, *The Pen Combined With Other Mediums* and *Pen and Ink in Illustration*, have been entirely re-written; and a short concluding chapter has been added. The greater part of Arthur Guptill's explanatory drawings as well as a good many examples of work by other artists have been retained. To this has been added almost a hundred examples of newer work. I am happy to have had a hand in again making this useful book available to students and lovers of the ink technique.

Henry C. Pitz

CONTENTS

DRAWING
with
PEN and INK

RONALD SEARLE
Illustration from "Paris Sketchbook"
The Saturn Press

SOME INTRODUCTORY CONSIDERATIONS

PEN DRAWING, as a separate and complete form of pictorial representation, is a thing of comparatively recent date, its greatest development having taken place since the beginning of the last quarter of the 19th Century.

This of course does not mean that pen drawing was unknown prior to that time. One has but to recall the illuminated manuscripts of the Middle Ages to realize with what skill pen lettering and certain types of decorative design were then done; but in this work the drawing was subordinated in nearly every instance to the lettering itself, or the pen lines in the illuminations were merely outlines or framework for the colored embellishments.

Again, if one brings to mind the many pen sketches and studies made centuries ago by some of the most famous of our old masters, it will be realized that the pen was turned to with great frequency even in their day. Analysis of their pen drawings makes plain, however, that this early work was usually in the form of preliminary studies for paintings or parts of paintings, or was much in the nature of a sort of pictorial shorthand, by means of which facts of interest were vigorously and sometimes, it must be admitted, rather crudely recorded. Apparently no attempt was then made to develop pen drawing as an art by itself, and it is only during the last few decades, as we have stated above, that this has been done. Today pen drawings are made not simply as adjuncts of another art or as means to certain ends, but as finished and complete things in themselves.

Undoubtedly the invention and gradual improvement of the various processes of photo-

mechanical reproduction, which have provided comparatively cheap and faithful methods for the reproducing of pen work, have afforded a great impetus to this development. Publishers have not been slow to take advantage of these processes and thus have created a demand for drawings in this medium, which artists in turn have hastened to meet.

Pen drawing has received encouragement, too, through the gradual perfection and standardization of the materials used—pens, inks and papers—of which an infinite variety may now

HEINRICH KLEY

be obtained easily at reasonable cost, permitting selections suitable for any purpose.

Even with these encouragements it is doubtful if pen drawing as an art would have so soon advanced to the enviable position it at present occupies had it not been for a realization on the part of the artists who contributed most to its development, that the pen, because of its peculiar qualities, was a medium demanding a far different treatment from that accorded any other.

It may be well to pause here for a moment for a consideration of certain fundamental principles which bear on all art work—principles with which these artists were undoubtedly familiar—and to see in what way they are applicable to pen drawing.

First, the reader should be reminded that each of the fine arts has certain restrictions as a result of which characteristic conventions have been developed. This thought will be amplified in a moment. Then too it is recognized that unless one bows to these restrictions, and accepts along with them such conventions as have been found naturally to accompany them, he is usually loading on to himself a heavy handicap so far as artistic accomplishment is concerned.

To illustrate the first thought: the sculptor, using plastic materials, is able to correctly copy many of the forms of nature, but is forced by his medium largely to disregard their color. The painter, on the other hand, can show their color, but, contrary to the worker in plastic materials, he is limited by his canvas to the delineation of only two dimensions, being forced to resort to conventionalities for the representation of the third. The worker in brush and wash of gray is forced still further to employment of convention, for he must interpret color in terms of various tones of gray, ranging from light to very dark. Such mediums as charcoal and crayon are frequently used in much the same way as wash,

adopting similar conventions. Yet these mediums may be employed in a linear manner, too, in which case new conventions come into play, particularly the use of outline and the suggestion of color, and of light and dark by means of various combinations of openly spaced lines. The pencil, though capable of being handled much like wash or charcoal or crayon, has also certain distinctive characteristics, notably its ability to hold a fairly sharp point. Each medium demands distinctive conventionalized treatment.

HEINRICH KLEY

MAE GERHARD

And now we come to the pen and its own limitations and conventionalities. Of both there are many, perhaps more than for any other medium. It might seem that this would put the pen at a distinct disadvantage, yet the ever-increasing popularity of pen work seems to indicate that the contrary is true. The pen is a linear tool, but unlike the crayon or charcoal or pencil it gives off no color or tone itself. Instead it serves as a vehicle of transmission of ink from bottle to paper, acting in this sense much like the brush. Unlike the brush, however, it has a rather fine and stiff point, capable of holding only a very small amount of ink, which makes it an impractical instrument for covering large areas of paper surface. This limitation acts in two direct ways. It tends to keep pen drawings somewhat small in size, and makes the use of a large variation of value in tone, as well as big areas of it, extremely difficult. It should be borne in mind that every line made with a pen is absolutely black (colored inks being a rare exception) against a background of paper which is usually white. This means that color must necessarily be disregarded altogether or suggested by the white of the paper or by various combinations of jet black lines. Tones of light and dark, too, must be ignored or suggested in similar manner. In order to build a value of gray it is necessary to dot the surface with stippling—a little used treatment—or to lay individual black lines side by side, or crossed in series. If one wishes subsequently to darken a tone obtained in one of these ways, he must painstakingly enlarge each existing line or dot or must put more lines or dots into the area. (Compare this with wash, by means of which it is possible to produce quickly and easily almost any given value, or to wash over and still further darken one.) To lighten a tone and still keep it in good character is practically impossible; if it is too dark there is nothing to do but erase (and in pen work this is far from easy) or put a patch on the paper and begin again.

It is because of these various technical difficulties of working with a fine point in black ink on white paper that it is so extremely hard, if not impossible, to build up values corresponding with all those in nature; it is for this reason that the less positive ones are disregarded, and the others simplified or merely suggested.

If color or tone is disregarded we must substitute something for it, unless the forms are to be lost; it is here that we resort to the conventionality of using outline, particularly where we wish one light object to stand out against another. The pen is an especially fine instrument for this outline work; not only is it unexcelled for the sharp delineation of shape and for precision of draftsmanship, but its lines, even though jet black, may be made very expressive of all sorts of irregularities of form and texture.

This use of outline, together with the method of tone building by means of lines or dots, as touched upon above, are two of the most distinctive characteristics of pen drawing. There are many minor conventions in use, to be sure, to which we are so accustomed that we hardly think of them at all; methods of suggesting shadow tones, for instance, and trees and clouds and the textures of building materials, and so on throughout a long list.

So these are the important restrictions and limitations and the resulting conventionalities of pen drawing—the facts which were recognized by those artists who made the art what it is, and which must still be recognized by those who would emulate them. If one tries to make a pen drawing larger than the instrument warrants, or attempts to carry gray tones all over his paper, or in any way disregards the peculiar properties of his medium, he will be forcing it to do that which it is not best adapted to do, and whatever success results from such methods is almost sure to be technical, rather than truly artistic.

This does not mean that one is so bound down that individuality is impossible; quite the contrary is the case, for it is often true that the more conventional the art the greater the opportunities for originality. We might go so far as to say that there is perhaps no medium offering one a better chance for the development of a personal technique, for pen drawing is akin to handwriting, and just as no two people write alike, so no two people draw alike.

We have already mentioned the popularity of pen work. Part of this is undoubtedly due to the methods of reproduction to which we have previously referred. Part of it, as we have said, is due to the ease and cheapness with which the necessary materials may be secured. Yet aside from all such causes pen drawing has made a lasting place for itself among the fine and applied arts through its intrinsic merits alone. Pen drawings, in their simple black against white, have a crispness and directness that are appealing; they are full of life and light. Many of them are only suggestive, leaving much to the imagination, and we take pleasure in this. A few lines here, and a few touches there, and sometimes that is all, yet there is a power to this suggestion which often makes photographs, telling everything, seem ineffective by comparison.

This virtue of line drawing over photography is realized even by "cold blooded" business men, or by the advertising experts representing them, as is evidenced by the great use of pen work for advertisements, even in a day when commercial photographers are existing on every hand.

Perhaps this popularity of pen work for advertising purposes has come about partly because reproductions of pen work harmonize so beautifully with the type matter of the printed page—due largely to their scale, their linear quality, and to the fact that they are printed on the same paper with the same ink. And this harmonious quality is undoubtedly one of the main reasons why pen illustrations for books and magazines and all sorts of similar press work are in such great demand.

It might seem that the strong contrasts of black and white in pen work would prevent such subtleties of representation as many subjects require, yet there is ample evidence in the form of drawings that this is not the case. In fact there is a delicacy to much pen work which is lacking in the work of other mediums.

Another point in the favor of drawings done with pen and ink, and one which should not be forgotten, is their cleanliness. Many mediums rub or soil easily, but pen drawings not only keep clean themselves, but do not soil other drawings with which they come in contact—and they do not fade.

Here, then, are some of the leading characteristics of pen drawing, some of the principles on which it is based, an outline of its history and certain uses to which it is put.

JOHN HUEHNERGARTH

DUFY

DRAWING MATERIALS

THE MATERIALS needed for pen drawing are few in number, simple, inexpensive, and easily obtained. Give a person two or three good pens and penholders, a bottle of ink and a pen-wiper, a few sheets of paper having a smooth, firm surface, a drawing board or some such support on which to place the paper, and a half-dozen thumbtacks with which to hold it there, a fairly soft pencil for constructing the drawing and a soft eraser for the later removal of the pencil lines and the cleaning of the sheet, a rather hard eraser or knife for the correction of pen lines, and he is well equipped for work of the usual sort.

The market is flooded with so great a variety of all such things that it seems necessary to offer some advice to the beginner in order to aid and restrict him in his selection. For the beginner, lacking guidance, is almost sure to purchase things of more diverse types and in larger quantities than is essential. If, instead, one buys but few things and learns to master them well, trying others only after this mastery has been attained, using greater and greater variety as added efficiency is gained—comparing, rejecting, substituting—he will eventually become partial to certain things especially suited to his own individuality. One should not, however, be too hasty or over-confident in his condemnation or rejection of materials; one would not heap blame upon a musical instrument simply because he found himself unable to perform on it at the first attempt. Like such instruments, materials often have hidden qualities that it takes long practice to bring into evidence.

One cannot hope to do good work with any but the best materials. Those recommended are by no means the only excellent ones, but as they have stood the test of time and have been held in favor by many leading artists, they are listed here without hesitation. If not available, others can perhaps be found that will give equal, and possibly even greater, satisfaction. Those listed should prove sufficient for most problems. A

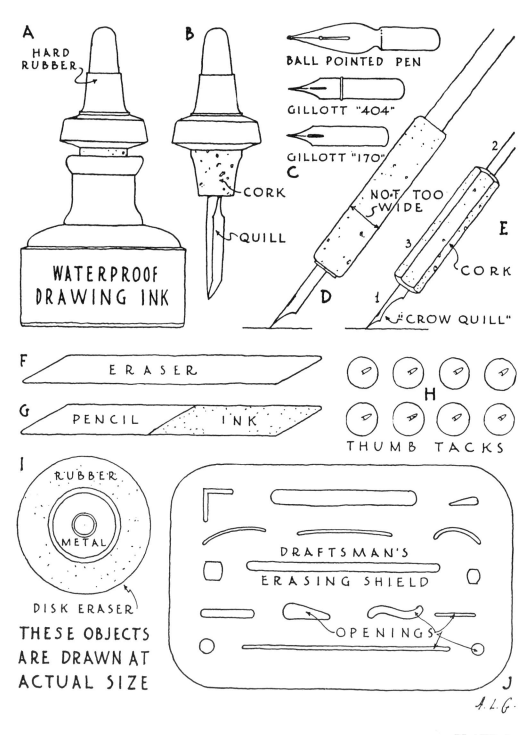

A HARD RUBBER

B CORK QUILL

C BALL POINTED PEN
GILLOTT "404"
GILLOTT "170"

D NOT TOO WIDE

E CORK

"CROW QUILL"

WATERPROOF DRAWING INK

F ERASER

G PENCIL INK

H THUMB TACKS

J RUBBER METAL

DISK ERASER

THESE OBJECTS ARE DRAWN AT ACTUAL SIZE

DRAFTSMAN'S ERASING SHIELD

OPENINGS

J

A. L. G.

PLATE 1.

few special things are described in later chapters, where their uses are also explained in some detail.

Pens—The choice of these is a matter of great importance, yet a matter concerning which artists themselves are so much at variance that it is small wonder that the student is at a loss to know where to turn.

Of metal pens there is no end. These are of early origin. Bronze pens were excavated at Pompeii, and we have other instances of their Roman use. These early pens copied the quill form, a form which we, today, find definitely suggested in our small "crow-quills" of steel, of which more will be said in a moment. Attempts were made to manufacture steel pens towards the close of the 18th Century, but it was not until 1825, in England, that Joseph Gillott made them practical, greatly improving their form and, by the introduction of machinery, cheapening their price. Even today Gillott pens still hold their place among the best made, and their fine and medium points seem to be in such general use among artists that we describe them first. One of the smallest of these, though not the smallest, is the "crow-quill" (659), a most delicate point, making an extremely fine line unless pressure is applied, when it will yield a line of astonishing width for so small a pen. Also very fine is the Gillott lithographic pen (290)—made for drawing on lithographic stone but popular for use on paper—and the Gillott mapping pen (291). This latter instrument is particularly facile for one so small, and is perhaps as well liked generally as any of the extremely fine ones. If not abused they will give a very fair length of service, but if repeatedly called into use for lines beyond their natural capacities they will soon fail. For the beginner such points are often dangerous, leading him into finicky ways. They are naturally better suited to small than to large work, and are at their best on smooth papers. The tiny Gillott tit-quill and the almost equally small No. 1000 and No. 2000 are finer than are needed for the usual forms of pen drawing. It is well for larger drawings, or for rougher surfaces, or for any lines but the finest, to turn to some such points as the Gillott 170, 303, or 404. These are better for all around work, particularly for the beginner. The 170 is fine enough for almost any purpose; the 303 is a very good medium size, while the 404 will give as coarse a line as is usually needed. No. 1, about the size of the 303, is recommended by the makers for flourishing and ornamental pen work. When pens larger than the 404 are required it is as well to turn to any of the makes commonly on sale.

There are two American manufacturers of drawing pens, Hunt and Esterbrook. Recommended Hunt pens are numbers 99, 100, 22, 56 and crowquill 102; Esterbrook pens are numbers 356, 355, 354, 358 and crowquill 62. Excellent pen points come from Brandauer, England—numbers 515, 517, 303 and crowquill 214.

A fine series of pens are the William Mitchell Fine Mapping Pens, made in England by British Pens Ltd. but also sold in this country. They are remarkably sturdy for all their delicacy of line. There are a dozen different points of differing degrees of firmness, all excellent—numbers 0157, 0530, 0565 and crowquill 0566 are recommended. One special pen made by this manufacturer, the Painter pen, is in my experience without a counterpart. This is a large pen of surprising delicacy and flexibility. It can range from a hair line to 1/16 of an inch in one stroke. It deserves to be better known. This company also makes a wide variety of lettering and music pens some of which are splendid for special kinds of ink drawing.

Fountain Pens—Fountain pens are more often used on sketching expeditions than in the studio.

Ball-point pens can be used but their line is characterless. The ink reservoir type is much better, a great deal depending upon the kind of tip used. Many of these pens offer a variety of tips but usually they are too stiff. An excellent pen made especially for drawing and lettering is the Osmiroid. It offers a wide variety of nibs, probably the most satisfactory for drawing are the Rolatip Series, ranging from Extra Fine to Broad, and particularly the Music nib, the most flexible of all. A good ink for these pens is Pelikan's Fount India.

For lettering, a ball, or oval, or dome pointed pen is good, and the same pen does for rather coarse lines of uniform width. For many types of decorative drawing, wide stubs such as are frequently used for lettering are practical. These may be had in many sizes. Then there are the round pointed or "spoon-bill" pens, also primarily intended for lettering; these are suitable for some types of pen drawing, particularly work of a very large or bold nature where lines uniform throughout their length are needed.

Penholders—As it is not uncommon for several pens to be employed on a single drawing, it is convenient to have several penholders, one for each of them. The crow-quill pens, and some of the other tiny points, require special holders, which may be purchased with them. One type is illustrated at "E," Plate 1. In this type the round barrel of the pen is pushed on to a stock of approximately the same diameter (2). A member (3) of cork slides down tightly to a convenient position, covering a bit of the upper end of the metal barrel. When the pen is not in use this member is pushed still further down to completely cover and protect the delicate point.

For the other pens, the forms of holder in general use for writing are satisfactory. In purchasing these see that they are sufficiently small in diameter to enter the neck of a bottle without touching it so that your hands can remain clean.

It is generally preferable to have the holders for the various pens of different colors, or individually marked by notches or in some such way, so that each may be easily identified at a glance. Thus a red holder might always contain a Gillott 303 pen, a brown one a 404, etc. One would soon become accustomed to this arrangement and it would save time when changing from one pen to another.

Penwiper—One should have a small chamois or felt, or some practical sort of wiper for his pens, and should keep them clean. Avoid one of linty character with loose particles to catch in the nibs, causing blots.

Ink—Most of the ink used for drawing is black and much of it is waterproof. Practically all is bottled in liquid form, though for many years artists purchased it in stick form, grinding it in water on a slate slab or similar rough surface until a sufficiently dark liquid was obtained. There are now many kinds on the market which are satisfactory. Well known brands are Higgins, Pelikan, Craftint, F. Weber and Co., Carter, M. Grumbacher, Speedball, Prang, and Winsor and Newton. Waterproof ink is essential when drawings are to be tinted with color or wet in any way. For other purposes where it is not to be exposed to moisture the ordinary black drawing ink is considered by many to flow better than the waterproof.

Whether the ink is black or colored, each bottle should be kept corked when not in use, as a prevention against thickening due to evaporation. At best the ink in a bottle is almost sure to become a bit gummy before it is gone. In this case it may be diluted a little according to the manufacturers' directions, though it is often well to buy a new bottle for the finer lines, saving the old for brush work or work with the larger pens.

Papers—Bristol board is one of the most com-

HENRY C. PITZ

Executed with Gillott's crowquill 659

monly used surfaces for pen drawing, and the better grades offer many advantages for this work. First of all it is smooth, which allows the pen to move over it in any direction without danger of the points stubbing in rough places. Again, it will stand a fair amount of erasing without serious injury (though erasing does frequently make it somewhat unsightly, destroying the gloss). It is firm enough to prevent minor irregularities of the surface under it, such as thumbtack holes in the drawing board beneath, from affecting it to any considerable degree—a great advantage over some thin papers, which can hardly be worked upon unless Bristol or other smooth board is placed under them. It stays quite flat, too, unless a great amount of ink is used when it sometimes shows a tendency to buckle. It is stiff enough so the finished drawings can be easily handled. As a rule both sides are alike so if one side is ruined the entire sheet is not wasted. It is produced in various weights, two or three ply being those customarily employed, the two being rather thin but doing well for most work, and the three an excellent thickness for almost any purpose. And it is not all of exactly the same surface but comes in different finishes, some very glossy, some smooth but only slightly shiny (and this is best for most problems) and some dull. There is also a kid-finish that is rather rough and therefore not as good as the smoother finishes for most pen work. We have touched on the fact that eraser marks show rather plainly, and this is especially true on the smoother grades. Likewise water makes dull spots of an unpleasant contrasting nature; also the board bends to form unsightly places if it is rolled and pressed or otherwise misused. Therefore, if the appearance of the finished drawing is important, it is well to protect the surface as much as is possible. When you buy, ask for a good make, one which is not too soft or absorb-

FRANCIS MARSHALL
from "An Englishman in New York"
G. B. Publications, Ltd.

RONALD SEARLE

ent, and then be sure that the sheets have not been bent or dented or otherwise damaged. Never allow Bristol board to be rolled tightly, if at all. If you carry it rolled under the arm, protect it from crushing if you wish it to keep its smooth appearance. One cannot be too careful of it.

If one wishes something which is damaged less easily, which stands erasing to better advantage, and which has a surface of a more interesting nature, let him try Whatman's hot pressed paper. This can be purchased in a form already mounted (ask for Whatman's hot pressed, mounted) or can be bought in sheets at smaller expense. These sheets may be used just as they are, or, as they have a tendency to wrinkle greater than that of Bristol board, they may be stretched onto a drawing board. One means of doing this is as follows. Choose a board at least an inch or two larger all around than the paper, and lay the paper loosely on this. With a sponge wet the paper thoroughly on the upper side, leaving about an inch of dry edge or margin all around. Allow the water to stand several minutes until the paper has swollen and buckled into a hilly surface. Then sponge off the superfluous water, leaving the paper just damp. As you complete this operation slightly dampen the previously dry margins; at once apply strong mucilage or glue to these margins; by the time this is on, the paper will have become fairly flat again, though still hilly. Next turn the paper upside down (it is best to have help with this), being careful not to get glue on the board anywhere under the sheet, and press the glued margins tightly to the board until they adhere all the way around. The paper will still be full of humps; as the edges are pressed down it can be drawn a bit smoother (do not pull it too hard for if too tight it will break when dry) and shrinkage as it dries will do the rest. If you make sure that the glued edges are kept fast by rubbing them down once or twice with your knife handle or some other convenient object, you will have, in a half-hour or less, a splendid surface of great strength: a surface showing injury or marks of erasing far less than Bristol board. Of course one must not extend his drawing onto the glued margins, as it is almost impossible to remove them whole when the rest of the sheet is cut from the board. Usually they are allowed to remain until later, when they are taken off at leisure by soaking thoroughly with water until they are soft, and may be washed or scraped off without trouble.

In addition to this Whatman's hot pressed paper there is another grade known as "cold pressed," somewhat rougher, as it is really a water color surface. Its roughness prevents pen work of the most perfect kind yet permits certain interesting effects, as all lines drawn upon it have a tendency to be irregular or broken. If pen drawings are to be tinted with color this is an especially good paper, though the hot pressed paper stands washes well too. In respect to wash application both of these papers have an advantage over Bristol board, which, with the exception of the kid-finished grade, is not well suited to such work.

Besides the Bristol boards and the Whatman's paper there are, of course, many other surfaces available which will take the pen well. Generally speaking such surfaces as are good for writing with a pen will do for drawing. The essential qualities to be sought are a fair degree of smoothness, coupled with sufficient firmness to prevent the stubbing of the pen or the blotting of the ink and to allow the use of an eraser or knife for corrections, without becoming absorbent or too unsightly in appearance. Some of the ordinary bond papers meet these specifications satisfactorily, especially those that come in the heav-

ier weights and in the better grades.

The architect and his assistants frequently use tracing cloth for the making of pen drawings, first dusting it with prepared powder as for ruled work and, of course, drawing on the dull side. The finished results may then be blueprinted, or prints in black and white, or brown and white, or red and white, may be obtained, printed in like manner. Another advantage of this material is that its translucency allows it to be used over a previously constructed layout, on which one may work as long as he wishes, the tracing cloth drawing being simplified in the final to a representation of the essentials. It is interesting to note, also, that the photo-engraver, when making reproductions, can work from a tracing cloth drawing as inexpensively and well as from one on paper.

Tracing papers of the stiffer grades are sometimes used in the same way, but whereas the cloth is strong and will stand almost any amount of erasing, the paper is easily torn or pricked through by the pen and can scarcely stand rubbing at all.

Drawing board—Almost any smooth drawing board of convenient size will do. It is best to have one large enough to afford some support to the hand in addition to the space given over to the paper, as one cannot do his best work in cramped space. If the board is at all rough it is advisable to put a few extra sheets of paper beneath the drawing paper, as a means of securing a smoother surface. If paper is to be stretched it is just as well not to use a new board, if an older one is available, as the stretching process, with its water and glue, may cause warping, slight raising of the grain of the wood, and a somewhat unsightly general appearance. Whether a board is old or new, that part of it beneath the "stretch" (as the stretched paper is called) should be washed beforehand to make sure it is clean; otherwise stains may come through the paper while it is damp, and show on the surface.

Thumbtacks—If paper is not stretched it is usually thumbtacked to the board. A dozen or so medium sized thumbtacks may be kept for this purpose, pressed into a convenient part of the drawing board when not in use.

Pencils—As most drawings are laid out in pencil before they are inked a few pencils are needed. On smooth Bristols, medium or rather soft grades are good, such as HB, B, or 2B, for rougher paper harder points like the F, H, or 2H are better.

Ruler—Whether or not a scale rule or such instruments as a T-square and triangles are needed depends on the nature of the work.

Erasers—There should be some kind of a soft or medium eraser for removing the pencil construction lines and for cleaning the entire sheet after the pen work is done. Art gum is excellent for this latter purpose and is one of the few erasers which can be used on smooth Bristols without destroying the gloss. If it is employed for the final cleaning of the sheet it will not lighten or gray the pen lines to the extent that many erasers do. This is important if a drawing is for reproduction. A harder eraser, perhaps one of the red or green ones, as shown at "F," Plate 1, is good for the more stubborn pencil lines and if employed patiently it will remove ink lines as well. The usual ink erasers such as pictured at "G" and "I," Plate 1, are too hard and gritty for most paper surfaces and should be used only with the greatest caution, if at all. The chemical ink eradicators will not remove most of the drawing inks.

Knife—Many artists prefer a good sharp knife or razor blade to anything else when it comes to making corrections. A knife is also a great convenience for many other purposes in connection with work of this kind.

Erasing shield—We illustrate at "J," Plate 1, a thin metal erasing shield of the type draftsmen use. Some such a shield is often almost indispensable when erasures are necessary, as it may be so placed on a drawing as to leave exposed to the action of the eraser only such portions of lines as are to be removed. If lines are unintentionally grayed by an eraser they should always be blackened again before reproduction is attempted. Gray lines sometimes show ragged edges, or even fail to reproduce at all.

Brush or cloth—The habit of dusting one's paper every few minutes is an excellent one, as it prevents the accumulation of bits of lint and the like which might get into the pen and cause blots. Use a soft brush or a lintless cloth for this.

Blotting paper—Some accidents are sure to happen; occasionally a bottle of ink is splashed or spilled, or a pen drips. Have a few blotters on hand for such an emergency.

ERIC FRASER

28

paper
bottle holder
(There are metal
holders available)

a holder for two
bottles made from
a box (extra holes
in cover for corks)

clip
another simple
one of heavy paper
or thin cardboard

Bottle holders—This danger from spilled ink is so real that some artists, in order to lessen it, use metal bottle holders which are on the market. Most of these holders are simply iron containers of sufficient weight to prevent easy overturning of the enclosed bottle (or bottles, as some take care of two or more). Though such a holder is by no means essential, the student, especially if he is inclined to be careless, will find himself relieved of considerable anxiety if his bottle is secured by something of the sort. Students in school, particularly when working in limited space, really need to take such precautions. It is not necessary that they go to the expense of buying holders, as homemade ink stands such as we suggest in the accompanying sketches do as well or better.

So much, then, concerning the selection and arrangement of the materials; next we must learn how to start to draw with them.

a cardboard
ink stand
holding two bottles
and several
pen holders

DANIEL VIERGE

PRACTICE IN PEN HANDLING

NOW COMES the time for starting the first actual work in pen drawing; work of the very simplest sort, designed to give one an acquaintance with his instruments and to provide for him a logical starting point from which to advance gradually and consistently, as broader perception and increased manual dexterity are gained.

The beginner must be cautioned not to try to rush ahead too fast; he must be content to master each step as he goes. Just as the student of the piano would find it impossible to render even the simplest composition completely and correctly until thoroughly drilled in the proper preliminary steps, so the student of drawing would find obstacles equally great if he allowed his impatience to lead him to an attempt of a finished drawing of any but the simplest of subjects until such rudimentary exercises as we have provided here had been fairly well mastered.

First of all he must acquire considerable facility in the manipulation of the pen itself, for without such facility satisfactory drawings cannot possibly be made.

It is easier for most of us to handle a pen than to manipulate a brush or a stick of charcoal or crayon, mainly because we are accustomed to its use in writing. Every bit of practice which one may have had in penmanship, or in writing with the pencil, for that matter, either in or out of school, will be of service. Drawing, however, requires a far greater freedom of movement than does writing. In writing the pen is held in very much the same position constantly; in drawing the position is frequently varied. In writing a comparatively small number of standardized curves and straight lines are combined in a methodical and oft repeated manner; in drawing there is almost no end to the variety in length and direction and character of the lines used or to the methods of combining them. The penman, then, seeks a certain monotonous perfection of stroke; the artist, on the other hand, must acquire the greatest possible versatility in the command of his instrument. He must be able to draw long, sweeping strokes, bold vigorous lines, crisp dashes and delicate dots. He must be able to draw reasonably straight lines and pleasingly curved lines, singly or in combination. And he must have the skill to draw all of these when and where he pleases on his paper, vertically, horizontally or slantwise. He must do so, too, with little conscious effort, so he can have his attention free to give to the development of his composition as a whole.

This does not mean that one must never attempt finished pen drawings until he has absolute control of his pen—a stage which he will doubtless fail to reach anyway. After what seems a reasonable amount of practice in drawing individual lines and in building simple tones (this amount depending on the natural aptitude and previous experience), the student should go directly to the making of drawings; in these he should continue his pen practice by varying his handling from time to time. He should also experiment with different pens and different papers, and with drawings of various sizes, in the meanwhile keeping up additional pen exercises at spare moments, scratching a few lines or building tones whenever opportunity offers, until a really worth while degree of proficiency has been arrived at.

Now just a word as to the materials for this first work. Not all of those described in the previous chapter are needed; the following are really essential.

1. Several sheets of smooth white paper or Bristol board of convenient size.

2. A medium pen or two such as the Gillott 303 and 404.

3. A penholder and a wiper.

4. A bottle of black drawing ink.

5. Drawing board or other suitable support.

6. A few pencils, thumbtacks and one or two erasers.

Most of the drawing Bristols are sold in sheets 22″ x 30″ or 22″ x 28″ or 23″ x 29″, so each sheet, cut in quarters, gives four sheets about 11″ x 14″ or 15″, a good size and proportion for most work of a preliminary character. We advise, too, that all paper used be cut to a uniform size, so far as possible, so the student will gradually form a collection of drawings which will fit well together either in exhibition or in a folio used for their protection. Above all, one should not try to economize by using too cheap a paper.

Thumbtack a sheet of your paper to a drawing board or, as a substitute, lay it on a stiff, firm book or similar support; the board is much the better of the two. Sometimes the paper, especially if it is a stiff Bristol, is laid on a smooth table top with nothing else under it. When a drawing board is employed its size is optional, though it is recommended that one not smaller than 16″ x 23″ be used; this is not only large enough for a half sheet of Bristol (about 15″ x 22″) but permits one to work on the quarter sheet without cramping.

When ready to draw, sit in a natural position. It is usually best to sit facing a table with the drawing board on top of it or resting against the edge, and so tipped as to permit the eye to view the entire paper easily. Be sure the sheet is well lighted, with the light falling from the left if possible. If the paper surface is shiny care should be taken that no harmful and disturbing reflection of light is thrown back into the eyes. Place the ink bottle in a convenient position, usually to the right so as to have it within easy reach, but not too near the edge of the table where it might be pushed off onto the floor. Next place a pencil or two and the pens and erasers nearby (and a blotter or rag handy for emergency) and you are ready to begin.

Try to hold the pen naturally, much the same as for writing (though, as we have already said, it will be necessary to vary its position to some extent for different types and directions of line, having it sometimes twisted or turned, sometimes almost vertical, and again more nearly horizontal). Keep the fingers far enough back from the point to prevent them from becoming daubed with ink. Above all do not cramp the fingers tightly onto the penholder.

Before starting the first lines place an extra paper (any clean sheet will do) under the hand to protect the surface of the drawing paper from dirt and moisture. Get the habit of working in this way from the start, seldom allowing the hand to touch the surface of the drawing.

Now dip your pen and confidently begin practicing the simplest types of lines. This does not mean to work hastily or carelessly; on the other hand an attempt should be made to have each line a thing of real feeling and beauty. Too often the beginner is misled by what seem to be carelessly drawn lines made by well-known artists. Lines of this sort are often the result of years of practice and usually very hard to imitate successfully. And remember that some well-known artists are famous in spite of their technique rather than because of it.

Straight lines offer a natural starting point for this practice. Turn to Plate 2 which shows a few practical straight line exercises. As this plate and those immediately following it have been reproduced at the size of the original drawings, and have not been corrected or touched up in any way, each stroke appears almost exactly as drawn.

Copy these exercises, starting with the horizontal strokes shown at "A." The arrows indicate the directions in which the original strokes were drawn, and the pen points show about the angles at which the pen was held. It is possible and proper to draw strokes like those at "C" in either of the directions indicated.

If you are left-handed you will naturally reverse most of these exercises, not only on this page but throughout the whole book. Left-handedness, by the way, is seldom a handicap in freehand drawing; some of our best artists are left-handed and at least one of our masters of the pen, Daniel Vierge, was forced, because of a stroke of paralysis, to change from his right hand to his left rather late in life and did so with little detriment to his style, once the adjustment was made.

Draw many strokes similar to those at "A," "B," "C," and "D." Vary their length and direction. Draw some slowly; some swiftly. Fill several sheets with them. Try different ways of holding the pen. Try different pens if you wish.

As you do these you will probably be able to discover some of your own weaknesses. You may have a tendency to run the lines which are intended to be horizontal up or down hill, or to tip your verticals. You may find it hard to start and stop your strokes just where you wish, or to keep them parallel. If these first troubles are yours it is perhaps because your paper is not directly in front of you, for if you do not look fairly at it you are almost sure to have difficulty. Get it right and then try again.

Following these exercises, done with comparatively even pressure of the pen, make strokes such as those shown from "E" to "P," tapering or shading each from dark to light or from light to dark. Work with care but do not expect too much mechanical perfection; notice that the ruled lines at "Q" are too straight and perfect to be interesting. Exercises like these will teach you some of the real capabilities of your pen.

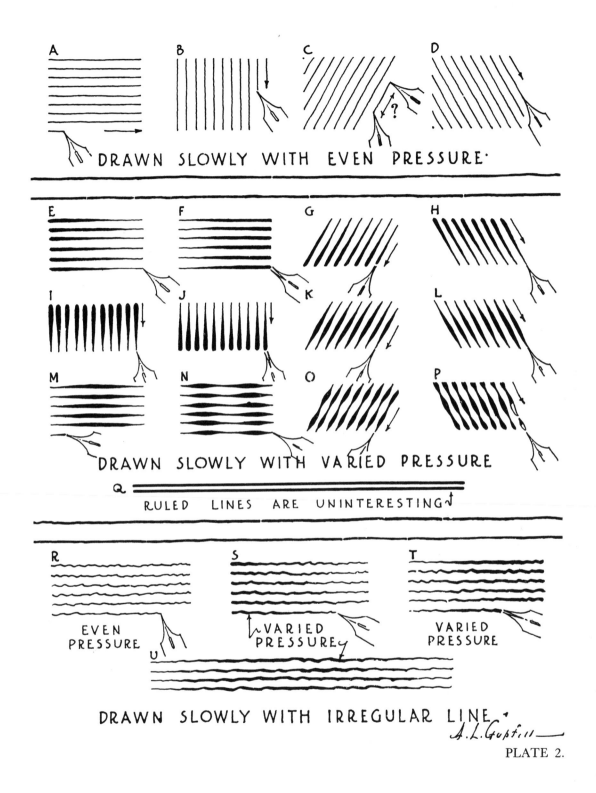

A B C D
DRAWN SLOWLY WITH EVEN PRESSURE·

E F G H
I J K L
M N O P
DRAWN SLOWLY WITH VARIED PRESSURE

Q RULED LINES ARE UNINTERESTING↓

R S T
EVEN PRESSURE   VARIED PRESSURE   VARIED PRESSURE
U

DRAWN SLOWLY WITH IRREGULAR LINE·

A.L.Gosfill

PLATE 2.

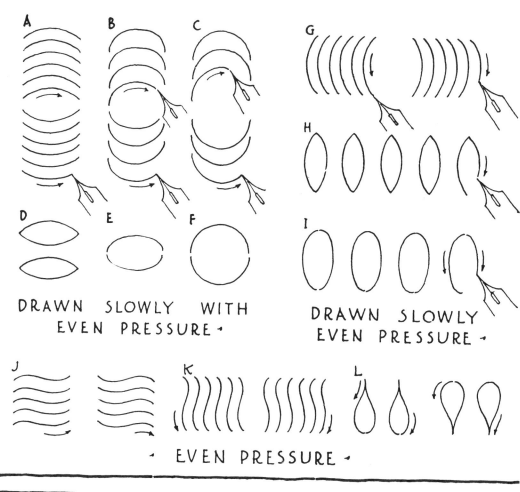

DRAWN SLOWLY WITH
EVEN PRESSURE ·

DRAWN SLOWLY
EVEN PRESSURE ·

· EVEN PRESSURE ·

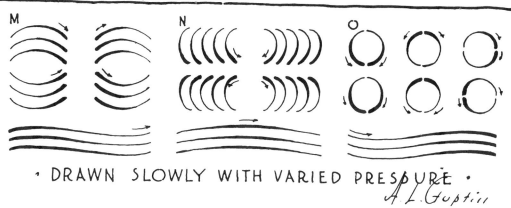

· DRAWN SLOWLY WITH VARIED PRESSURE ·

A. L. Guptill

PLATE 3.

Sometimes an evident shake or tremor to a line is highly desirable, so make irregular lines also, such as those at "R," "S," "T," and "U," straight in general direction, some long and some short, some with even and some with varied pressure, and at different slants.

Now turn to Plate 3, which shows a variety of curved lines. This page speaks for itself. Here again, copy these exercises and then devise others of your own. These were drawn slowly; draw some similar strokes quickly. Copy other strokes from pen reproductions, too; hunt and see how many types you can find.

When you have made many kinds of individual lines, over and over again, and think you are getting the "feel" of your pen, you are ready to turn to the next chapter, dealing with the combination of strokes into tones.

In leaving this chapter, however, keep the thought in mind that whenever you get the opportunity you should come back to practice the sort of thing which is suggested here.

KNIGHT

EDWARD SMITH

OUTLINE

ACTUAL OBJECTS have no true outlines—no definite edges or profiles bounding them which appear as lines. We see one object as distinct from others only because it is lighter or darker, or of a different color, or has shade or shadow tones upon it or about it, or other effects of illumination which define it or detach it from its surroundings. If the reader has doubtful inclinations regarding the truth of this he has only to examine objects with an unprejudiced eye. In some instances he will find what at first glance may appear to be outlines, but analysis will prove them to be nothing but extremely narrow areas of tone—either light or shade or shadow or perhaps color.

Despite the truth of this assertion, the fact remains that it is very hard for us to think of objects as not bounded by definite lines, or, to state it conversely, it is remarkably easy for us to think of objects as though they were actually bounded by definite lines.

If one draws these imaginary boundary lines of some object, and adds similar lines showing the separation of one part (or tone or color) of the object from another, he has on outline drawing of the object. As this is a comparatively simple and natural process it does not seem an overstatement to say that the employment of outline offers the easiest and most natural form of pictorial delineation.

Pen and ink, because of its ready adaptability to linear representation, is the most logical medium for the drawing of outline; nothing excels it for the sharp delineation of form and precision of draftsmanship.

The artist knows that if he is to express all that he may desire, and express it well, he must learn to use many kinds of outline, ranging from the most direct to the most subtle. He realizes that there must be a definite relationship between the type of line drawn and the size and character of the subject pictured, as well as the size and purpose of the drawing itself. He works to master the technique and use of lines.

MAE GERHARD

The simplest of the outlines which we have in pen work is that employed at "1," Plate 4. This is a line of approximately uniform thickness throughout, entirely bounding each object depicted, being, therefore, a true "out" line or outer line—a profile. Other examples are shown at "2" (Figures "J" and "L") on the same plate. Such a line is sometimes quite satisfactory for representing extremely simple objects of expressive contour, or those which are flat or low in relief, or even solid or rounded forms whose characteristics are already well known to us. It makes little difference whether the forms are geometric like those at "1" ("A," "B," "C," "D," etc.) or irregular like the tree shape at "G."

Architects often use simple contour lines to express the cross-sections of individual mouldings, as at "H," or of groups of mouldings such as those forming the cornice at "I."

For most purposes, however, such meagre "out" line work is insufficient and needs to be supplemented with enough additional line work, within the forms bounded by the profile lines, to render the whole understandable and interesting. At "K" and "M," for example, lines have been added within the leaf forms outlined at "J" and "L," and the resulting sketches tell a more complete and satisfactory story.

This at "K" and "M" is the most common simple form of outline drawing—a line bounding each object, with additional lines within to mark off or define every essential portion and to give adequate expression to the whole, all the lines being of approximately one width. This kind of work is applicable to many types of subjects, and the student is advised not so much to copy these drawings as to select subjects which appeal to him, either objects or photographs (making sure that they offer good variety of practice), and to draw them in this general manner. Plate 1, on equipment, was done by this method, all

the lines but the margins having been drawn with a Gillott 303 pen.

A bit later we shall offer a few special instructions for the architectural student or draftsman. Just now we wish particularly to urge him to practice this simple form of outline work as it is excellent preparation for office practice, where the draftsman is often called upon to draw ornament or mouldings or to do lettering of a type which will harmonize well with the instrumental portions of architectural drawings. The draftsman should use not only the customary types of drawing papers and boards but should, in addition, practice on tracing cloth and tracing paper, working for clean-cut lines, as they are the type that blueprints well. It seems advisable, in passing, to mention that even the instrumental portions of almost all architectural drawings are of a very similar form of outline work to this under present consideration, each object being either fully represented by instrumental outline or adequately suggested by some conventional indication. This thought is amplified and illustrated later on.

Though the kind of freehand outline drawing so far described (in which lines of uniform width are used) is suitable for many architectural purposes, and excellent wherever an extremely simple expression of objects is sufficient, it offers too little variety to serve more than a limited purpose. At "N," Plate 4, we show another kind of work, in which two widths of line are used instead of one, the work sometimes being done by the previous method first, and a wider profile added later. This, again, is a method of working quite common to architectural subjects where it is desired to give the greatest emphasis to some object or detail as a whole rather than to its parts. When architectural drawings of this type are to be blueprinted, they are made on tracing cloth or paper, and diluted ink, which blue-

A

C

E

G

B

D

F

H   I

TRUE "OUT" LINE
DRAWING

1

N   3   J   K   2

TWO   WIDTHS   OF   LINE

O   P

L

ACCENTED   OUTLINE

M

HAT HAT

Q   R

S   T

SUGGESTIVE OUTLINE
AND BROKEN OUTLINE

LINES ALL OF ONE
WIDTH

A.L.G.

PLATE 4.

39

prints somewhat indistinctly, is sometimes substituted for black ink for the fine lines, the coarse ones remaining black. This naturally results in still greater contrast in the prints than would be obtained by the two widths of line alone.

One should not assume, from the above, that this method of using two widths of lines is applicable only to the architectural form of work, for the use of two or even more widths is common to many other classes of work, particularly decorative drawing.

We next turn to a type of outline work which is far more subtle than either of these so far considered, a type often referred to as "accented outline." In this type the lines vary in width and character so as to express more fully the objects represented. At "P," Plate 4, is a bit of Gothic ornament based on the grape. This was first done in simple outline. Next, some of the lines, especially those below and to the right of every projecting portion, were darkened to suggest the shadows, thus adding to the sense of relief. Many of the lines were accented at their points of junction too, notice the grapes in particular. This not only suggests the natural darkness which might exist at such points but tends to make the drawing "snappy" and interesting. In the little sketch at "O" similar accents at "1" and "2" show very plainly. No definite rules can be given for the placing of such accents; it is all a matter of natural feeling plus observation and practice.

Still more subtle, and for many purposes more realistically suggestive, and consequently more valuable, is the type of accented outline work shown at "S" and "T," Plate 4. Here there was no continuous or definite pen outline drawn. If you study the word "Hat," at "Q," it will be seen that each letter is surrounded by outline. At "R" the same word is shown with about half the outline omitted, yet we are still able to read the word; the reader supplies the missing parts through memory and imagination. To thus suggest or indicate brings more interesting and more artistic results in many cases than does tiresomely complete outline. In literature or the drama we like those things best, as a rule, which were written with the assumption that we have some intelligence ourselves. Those of us who employ linear drawing as our medium of expression should give those who view our creations credit for equal readiness of comprehension. Now, turning again to the leaf at "S," and the sweet pea at "T," we see that part of the outline is omitted, part of it suggested by broken or dotted lines and part drawn with lines varying in width; we see, too, that many small accents of black are added at the junctures of the lines. This suggestive and broken type of accented outline is perhaps one of the most common in all pen work. Its importance is such that it should be conscientiously studied and practiced.

Plate 5 shows an application of the same types of line to the drawing of objects. At "1" the small box was drawn with lines of uniform width. At "2" the same box was drawn with accented outlines. Notice that by making the lines heavier towards the front of the box (A) it seems to come forward. Notice, too, that by allowing the table line to fade away as it approaches the box (B) it appears to pass behind the box, remaining in the background. At "3" the same box is shown with a delicate broken outline such as might be needed to indicate a rough cloth or leather covering. In Sketch 4, at "A," a metal pitcher is shown with the outline partly omitted and the rest sketchily suggested. The dark line beneath serves to set it down firmly onto the table. Crisp, sharp lines are usually the best for expressing smooth metal or glass objects. When we have softer textures, such as those of the book at "B," a greater variety of line is needed, there-

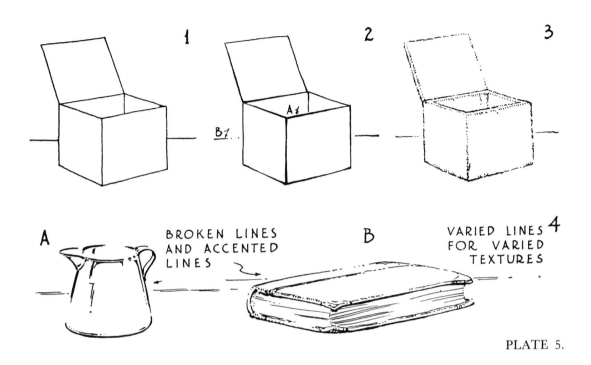

1

2

3

A   BROKEN LINES
AND ACCENTED
LINES

B   VARIED LINES 4
FOR VARIED
TEXTURES

PLATE 5.

fore, objects of this sort are particularly fine subjects for drawing. In fact the student should seek the widest possible variety in his subjects. Generally speaking beautiful things should be sought, for in many ways more is gained from studying beautiful things than ordinary things. But the artist cannot always draw beautiful things; he must be sufficiently versatile to handle any and every sort of subject. He must be able, above all, to represent the individuality of his subject, whatever it may be. Consequently it is often well for the student to select some object which has a strong individuality; certain characteristics of its own which demark it from other objects. If beautiful, so much the better. It should not be merely "pretty," however, and some objects which are in a sense positively ugly are so full

of character as to be well worth drawing. The author feels that he personally gained a stronger grasp of the essentials of pictorial delineation through the drawing of old worn out shoes and hats, dilapidated books and antique dishes, which were battered to the point of appearing entirely useless for any purpose, than from any other type of subject. If one learns to look for the individual characteristics of each subject and to picture them to advantage he gains a real power of analysis and of expression.

In this chapter we have discussed types of outline drawing but have said nothing about the method of actually laying out the freehand work, for, as we have already mentioned, it is presupposed that the reader is sufficiently familiar with freehand sketching to do the pre-

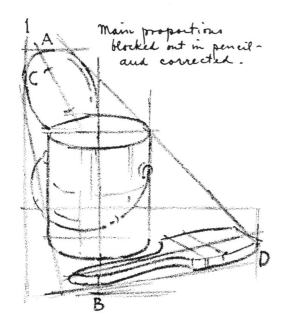

1 A C — Main proportions blocked out in pencil — and corrected. B D

2 — Smaller subdivisions added and corrected.

FIRST STAGE (PENCIL ONLY)   SECOND STAGE (MORE DETAIL)

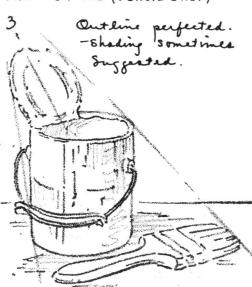

3 — Outline perfected. —shading sometimes suggested.

4 — Outline inked. Ready for erasing of pencilling and final correction of ink lines.

THIRD STAGE (PENCILING COMPLETED)   FOURTH STAGE (OUTLINE INKED)

PLATE 6.

42

paratory pencilling which is customary before the inking is started. There can be no harm, however, in reviewing the usual method of procedure for the benefit of the beginner. Let us turn to Plate 6 for a moment. Here at "1" is a first stage drawing of some simple objects, done in pencil. The first lines drawn were those at "A," "B," "C" and "D." These located the extremities of the entire mass upon the paper. Next the objects were sketched in a simple manner, the general proportions being worked over and corrected until satisfactory. In the second stage sketch shown at "2" more detail was added in pencil, the smaller proportions being studied until they, too, were right. The third stage at "3" is simply a natural further development of the whole thing, the pencil lines being carried to completion. At "4" the outline has been inked and the drawing now stands ready for the erasure of the pencil work, and the final touching up of the pen lines, which may be finished in any of the manners just described. The same method of procedure would be used for other types of subjects, each drawing showing a logical advance from the simple beginning to the completed results.

If one is not interested in the drawing of such things as we have shown—flowers, fruit, ornament, books, dishes and the like—he may make selections of any kind of subject so long as it offers him good practice. Buildings or parts of buildings are favored by many. These may be done in very simple outline or, if the student is sufficiently advanced, they may be handled in a more complicated way, and still the results may remain outline drawings in spirit. In connection with the drawing of buildings, the student is referred to Plate 7. In Sketch 1 (B) is a suggestion in outline of the top of a chimney; the simplest sort of representation. At "A" is a somewhat more elaborate study in which the outlines

of some of the bricks and other building materials give to the whole an effect of light and shade. "C" shows how such a subject might be interpreted by free methods of light and shade work. At "D" is a portion of a stone wall; here the effect of masonry is obtained by outlining the separate stones with accented outlines, the darker lines suggesting the shadows cast by the stones in the mortar joints.

Sketch 2 shows a different treatment in the drawing of a porch corner of an old house on Long Island. This is less suggestive of form, for here every visible architectural member has been definitely outlined, the projecting portions being still further strengthened by the addition of heavier profile lines.

Sketch 3 is another which stands on the dividing line between complex outline and simple shaded work. The lines, which give the effect of shading, are mainly outlines indicative of the irregular course of shingles, the branches of the trees and the scattered masses of foliage. To these were added touches of solid black in the windows and under the cornices to emphasize the center of interest.

Whereas Plate 7 shows architectural subjects only, they are not of a sort exclusively interesting to architects or their assistants. Plate 8, on the other hand, was drawn with some of their particular requirements in mind. Sketch 1 shows at "A" a typical small-scale instrumental elevation of a double-hung window. We have already pointed out that such architectural work as this is really outline drawing, and whether we have a small detail as here or the working drawings of an entire building, this is still true. The architect and draftsman become so accustomed to thus working in outline instrumentally that it is natural and easy for them to interpret subjects by freehand means in a somewhat similar manner, using lines of a crisp, clean-cut character.

1

A

B

C

D

2

3

The Mulford House (1660)
Easthampton Long Island

A.L.G.

PLATE 7.

44

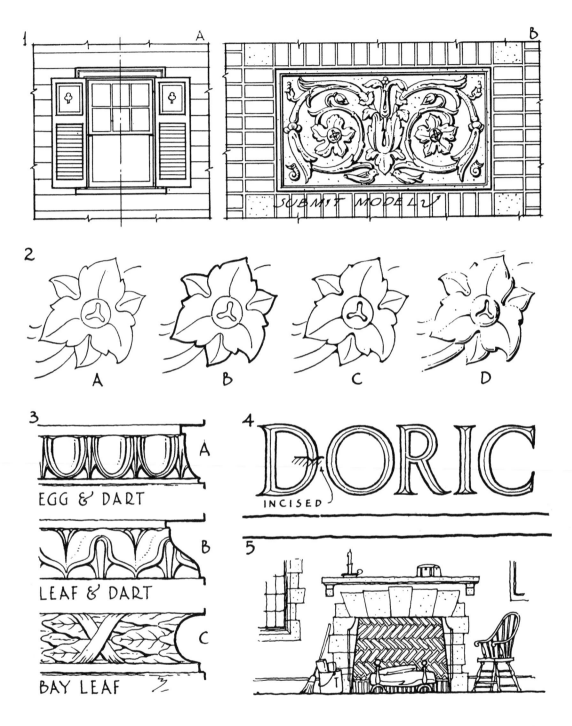

1

A

B

SUBMIT MODELS

2

A   B   C   D

3

A
EGG & DART

B
LEAF & DART

C
BAY LEAF

4
DORIC
INCISED

5

PLATE 8.

Freehand drawings so done harmonize nicely with instrumental work; a freehand outline elevation or perspective of a house, for instance, is harmonious with the instrumentally drawn plans.

Frequently the draftsman is called upon to do freehand work in direct conjunction with instrumental line work, particularly in the drawing of ornament. It is very important, therefore, as we have said before, for the draftsman to learn to make clean-cut freehand lines. He should know how to do this on both paper and tracing cloth. By tracing good ornamental forms on the linen, in pen and ink, two objects are accomplished at the same time, for facility in freehand drawing is acquired and a knowledge of ornament is gained, both essential parts of an architect's training. Sketch 1 shows at "B" an example of the type of work in which clean-cut freehand lines are used in conjunction with ruled lines. This is a common type of work, though more often in working drawings, especially if at small scale, the freehand lines are uniform in character rather than accented as in this example. In large scale work, however, and particularly in full size detailing, modelling is often suggested in this or some similar accented way. In fact, draftsmen frequently fall back to the methods of outline drawing which we have described already and which we now illustrate again in Sketch 2. At "A" we have drawn a rosette with uniform lines; at "B" we have silhouetted it with a heavy outline to give emphasis; at "C" we have used the uniform line but have accented most of the points of junction indiscriminately; at "D" we have used broken and suggestive forms of accented outline indicating light and shade, with a few other lines added to increase the effect of the modelling of the parts.

In Sketch 3 we show several mouldings in accented outline; needless to repeat, these are very important subjects for the draftsman, as are the many types of architectural lettering, one of which we illustrate in Sketch 4.

Sketch 5 shows a treatment not uncommon in architectural practice, for here the little interior was first laid out instrumentally in pencil and was then inked freehand, the pencil lines being finally erased, bringing about a result having much of the accuracy of instrumental work plus some of the sketchiness of freehand work.

Students not interested in architecture should hunt, as we have mentioned, for examples of published outline drawings which do interest them; the magazines and papers are literally full of them—fashion drawings, caricatures, advertising sketches, decorative drawings, etcetera. The beginner should pick simple ones and study them, trying similar ones himself. He should avoid those which are too complex, as complicated outline drawings are often more difficult to do than simple shaded ones. In any case he should remember that no matter how simple or how complex the subject may seem, it should be drawn accurately; the fewer the lines to be used the greater the need for accuracy.

When one has learned to handle outlines which are comparatively simple, he should turn to elementary shaded work, later turning back to outline and applying it to the representation of more difficult subjects.

LYLE JUSTIS

TONE BUILDING

IN PEN WORK, as we have pointed out, each line or dot made is pure black, and usually on white paper; when an effect of either light or dark gray is desired it is obtained only by placing dots or lines of pure black close together so as to produce a result which appears gray. The process of thus learning to suggest grays of different tone, and at the same time to indicate textures of numerous sorts, is very fascinating. Innumerable combinations of many kinds of dots and lines are possible. The student should start with some of the simpler ones such as are shown on Plates 9 and 10 and should later try many experiments of his own.

Before practice is started let us turn to the illustrations for a moment. In the first marginal sketch on this page, lines have been drawn with a medium pen (Gillott 303) 1/8 of an inch apart in a space one inch square. In the next sketch below, the same pen has been used but the lines are 1/16 of an inch apart; in the sketch below that, twice as many lines occupy the same area. In the other series of three sketches there is a disposition of lines similar to those in the first three sketches but the effect is darker because the lines are drawn with a heavier pen point, (Esterbrook oval point 788).

As the eye passes down these two sets of sketches it is conscious of lines in the upper ones but in the lower ones the lines, although just as distinct, have begun to merge into a tone. This is the basis of most ink tones.

For a second and similar example, compare Plate 9 with Plate 2, and it will be seen that the four squares of tone at "1," "2," "3," and "4" are practically the same in formation as the groups of lines at "A," "B," "C," and "D." Here, again, the main point of difference is that in Plate 9 the various parallel lines in each group are kept so close together that they tend to merge into a unified whole.

Tones such as these, built up of straight lines, are among the most common used in pen work, and, being the easiest to do, afford a good starting point for the beginner, who should commence his practice by copying the examples at the top of Plate 9. As a general rule it is well to make the strokes approximately 1/32 of an inch apart. Do not measure, however, for there should be nothing of the mechanical about such exercises, as in actual pen drawing the spacing depends on many things and is usually variable. It is generally worse to get lines too close together than too far apart, for unless a reasonable distance is left between them they may blot or run

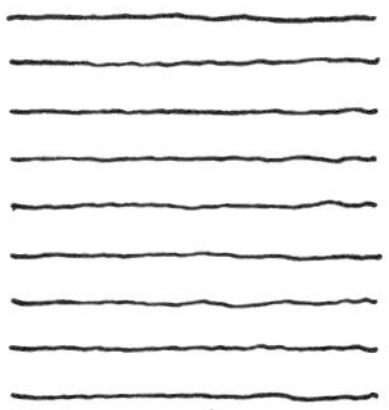

1/8" spacing (medium pen)

1/16" spacing (medium pen)

1/32" spacing (medium pen)

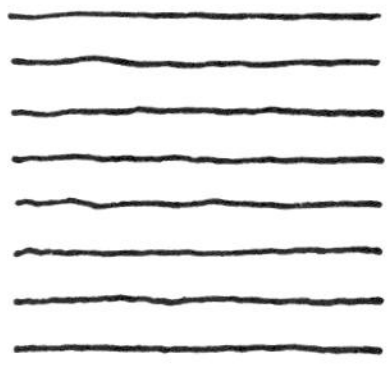

1/8" spacing (coarse pen)

1/16" spacing (coarse pen)

1/32" spacing (coarse pen)

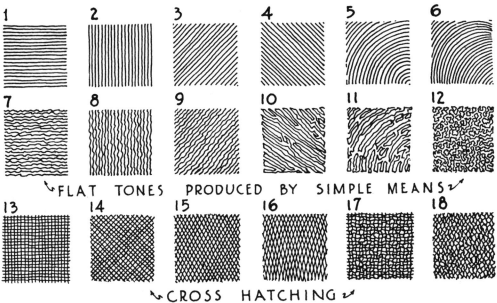

FLAT TONES PRODUCED BY SIMPLE MEANS

CROSS HATCHING

• DRAWN SLOWLY WITH EVEN PRESSURE •

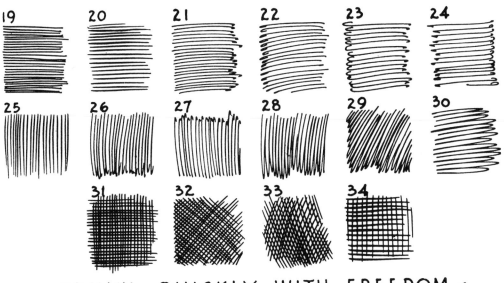

• DRAWN QUICKLY WITH FREEDOM •

(COMBINE CURVED STROKES ALSO) A. L. Guptill

PLATE 9.

49

together in places, which is often objectionable. Particularly when the work is planned for reproduction, the lines must be quite openly spaced, as most drawings are reproduced at reduced size with proportionate diminution of all the spaces. This means that if the work is not sufficiently "open" the cuts from which the reproductions are made may fill with the printers' ink, causing smudgy results.

The student should practice drawing many of these small areas of tone, keeping the lines evenly spaced so as to give a uniform grayness or flatness to each. He should draw them with lines slanting in various directions, and with curves as at "5" and "6," Plate 9. He should try different pens and papers.

When a fair facility in the making of these even lines is gained, a greater variety of line should be practiced, for aside from indicating different tones one must learn to suggest various textures, and this demands an acquaintance with the greatest possible variety of lines and tones. The squares from "7" to "11," Plate 9, are much like those from "1" to "5," excepting for the wavering or wandering quality of the lines. At "12" is an extreme example of the type of line which wanders, changing direction to such an extent that the tone scarcely seems made up of lines at all. It is worth observing that in this tone variable areas of white, about 1/32 of an inch wide, do actually separate all parts of the wandering lines.

One should not only practice all these exercises but should hunt for other examples of tones and invent some of his own, remembering, when copying reproductions, that the apparent fineness and close spacing of lines is often the result of great reduction from the sizes of the originals.

Such work as we have suggested will soon give one a reasonable dexterity in filling small areas with simple tone. The student will find that he is able to control the degree of darkness of each area in two ways—first by varying the distances between the lines and second by differing the widths of the lines themselves. The artist needs this knowledge constantly; if he builds a tone of gray and finds it too light in effect, when finished, he may darken it by adding more lines between those already drawn or by widening the existing ones. In the first instance the tone becomes more homogeneous; in the second the lines themselves grow somewhat more prominent. This is sometimes of advantage, especially when the lines suggest some particular texture; contrarily it is often of equal disadvantage when they do not.

The tones to which we have so far referred are of the type which might be called "open"; each stroke is a fairly definite and complete thing. For many kinds of work such tones are eminently satisfactory. There are some purposes better served by other types, and among these, those made up by crossing lines (or "cross-hatching" as it is called) have their occasional place. Though not recommended for too frequent use they are worth practicing. From "13" to "18," Plate 9, we have shown several examples of cross-hatching which explain themselves.

In the lower half of the sheet are tones built up with far greater freedom; these are perhaps more typical of most of those used in pen work than are the others above, yet all kinds are important. These tones were formed very quickly, and in copying them the student should not expect to duplicate them exactly; instead he should work for their general effect. He should try others of his own, too, using curved lines as well as straighter ones, varying weight and length of lines and trying tones consisting of tapered strokes, like those previously discussed in describing Plates 2 and 3. He should gain as much versatility in pen handling as he can.

JOSEPH CLEMENT COLL

At this stage the student should be able to draw a large variety of individual strokes and to combine them into small areas of tone. It is easier and more satisfactory to do this than to cover the larger and somewhat irregular areas as is necessary in most drawings. Hence the next move is to attempt this very thing.

51

The upper half of Plate 10 is designed to show a few of many practical combinations of lines. Those at "1," "2," "3," and "4," require little explanation. The arrows are directed to the lines or, more properly, spaces of junction between the various groups of strokes. In grouping lines in this way, care should generally be taken to make these points of junction as inconspicuous as possible. Tones "6," "7," "8" and "9," Plate 10, should be compared with "1," "2," "3," and "4," as they are very similar. These largely disguise or do away with the junction lines just mentioned, through the use of greater variety in length and direction of stroke. Tones "5" and "10" show interesting slanting interruptions to the straight vertical and horizontal lines. This sort of thing is very useful for some purposes, especially where a large area of tone has a tendency to become monotonous in character. The lines dragged across Tone "6" serve a similar purpose. The tones from "11" to "15," inclusive, were drawn with great freedom; these would be particularly useful in the representation of rough textured objects of many kinds.

As in previous examples, the student should practice these tones. He should seek out others from available pen drawings and reproductions and copy them over and over, besides carrying on experiments of his own along similar lines.

In drawings of a highly conventional nature or decorative quality, such tones as those at the lower half of Plate 10 are often seen, tones which not only give the desired value of light and dark but which also show some special texture or pattern. Though interesting, they are of less importance to the student at this time than are those shown above, with the exception, perhaps, of the spatter tones shown at "16," "17" and "18," and the stippled tone at "19." This latter was made by dotting the entire surface with fine dots of the pen, care being taken to avoid the

stiff effect that might follow were they arranged in straight lines. Such a tone is often most useful; distant hills or mountains may be expressed by it, as well as such rough surfaces as stone or stucco walls. For similar purposes the spatter tones are good, too. These may be done in several ways; in all of them it is necessary to cover first such portions of the paper as are to be kept free from the spatter.

If the areas to be spattered are simple in shape, even and true, the rest of the paper can be easily protected by strips of heavy paper or cardboard; stencil board is excellent. When the shapes to be hidden are irregular in shape, and consequently harder to cover with paper, pure artists' rubber cement is sometimes painted directly onto the parts to be protected. After the inking is done (this will be explained in a moment) the cement is rolled off by the fingers without injury to the paper. Impure cements must be avoided, as they stain paper. Some artists employ, for covering drawings during spraying operations, what is known as frisket paper. This is a somewhat transparent, or, more properly, translucent paper, which is coated with rubber cement and then pressed down over the entire drawing, after which the frisket is cut with a sharp knife or razor blade to the exact outline of the parts to be spattered, and the unwanted portions stripped off, the finger being next rubbed over the exposed portion of the drawing surface in order to remove any remaining cement. After this the spattering is done.

Heavy tracing paper is often used as a substitute for the frisket, being cut out with the razor blade in the same way, and then held down by rubber cement or pins or small weights placed along the edges. As the tracing paper may wrinkle from the dampness of the ink, care must be taken to see that none of the ink spray is spattered under it.

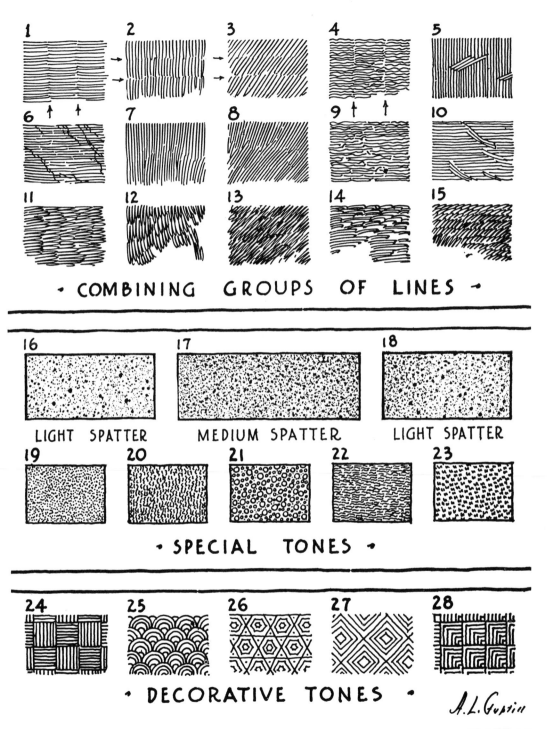

· COMBINING   GROUPS   OF   LINES ·

LIGHT SPATTER   MEDIUM SPATTER   LIGHT SPATTER

· SPECIAL   TONES ·

· DECORATIVE   TONES ·

A.L.Gustin

PLATE 10.

When the paper has been properly prepared, in some such manner as we have described, a scheme for the spattering must be decided on and carried out. These are several practical methods. In one of them a toothbrush is so dipped in the black ink that each bristle is inked for an eighth-inch or so. Some prefer to ink the brush by rubbing the bristles with the quill of the ink bottle stopper. Then, with the brush held nearly horizontally in the left hand, bristles up, the student strokes the bristles towards him with a wooden match or toothpick, causing them when released to snap or catapult tiny drops of ink onto the exposed paper until it has been sufficiently darkened. Too much ink in the brush will naturally cause blots, so it is best to try the process on waste paper before risking the drawing. Another method is to rub the ink-charged brush, bristles down, over a piece of wire screen held a couple of inches or so above the drawing, previously placed flat or nearly flat. This method perhaps offers the artist somewhat better control over his medium.

These somewhat lengthy explanations of methods of stippling and spattering tones are enough to show that such work is not easily done. The stippling is the simpler of the two methods if the areas to be covered are small and by varying the sizes of pens it is possible to vary the stippled effects in very interesting ways. One

has better control over the stipple; the more dots the darker the tone, of course. Graded effects are easy to obtain. There are several dangers from spattering: first, it is hard to judge the value of the tone correctly, and easy to get it too dark; second, it is difficult to keep from getting some of the tiny drops of ink under the frisket or protecting paper; third, it is easy, if one becomes impatient, to blow or spatter so many small drops onto the drawing that they run together and form blots before they have time to dry. It is well to stop for a few moments now and then to give the ink a chance to dry. In spite of these difficulties, which a little experience will overcome, spattering is much quicker than stippling for large surfaces, even though more preliminary work is necessary. Once the spattering itself is begun it progresses very rapidly.

Before leaving this subject it seems best to issue a word of warning, particularly to the beginner. This is, that these expedients, stippling and spattering, are not truly pen drawing. They produce results so different in character from the customary forms of pen work that if used injudiciously or to excess they are almost sure to cause trouble. Have them in mind, however, and try them occasionally. In the meantime gain the greatest possible proficiency in the combination of true pen strokes.

VALUE STUDY

VALUE is an important word in the artist's vocabulary. Let us see what this word really means. In its customary significance outside of the realm of art the word relates, as we know, to the desirability or worth of a thing, sometimes to its utility or to its market price. In the world of music it refers to the relative length of a tone as signified by a note. Its use in art is similar to its use in music, only, instead of referring to the relative length of a tone, it refers to the relative amount of light or dark in some given area. If an object is light in color or tone, for instance, we say that it is light in value; if dark in color or tone we call it dark in value; if of medium tone we pronounce it of middle value.

In pen drawing, if we wish to represent an object which is light in value we usually do so—though there are exceptions—by employing tones which are also light in value. If we wish to picture some very dark object in a natural way we use values that are dark. If our desire is to show the appearance of a dark red apple against a light yellow background we use values of dark and light closely approximating the amount of dark and light in the objects themselves. However, because of the technical limitations of the pen, which make it difficult to show all the possible range of values from the white of the

paper to the black of the ink, we frequently considerably simplify actual values in their representation. Light objects, for example, are often shown as white, and dark ones as black, and if objects have a large number of slightly varying tones which do not seem wholly necessary to the satisfactory pictorial expression of the objects, these tones are simplified in the representation, only the general values of each mass being expressed.

In the making of a pen drawing—or any sort of picture for that matter—it is not the absolute correctness of each individual tone that is most important (though no one can doubt the usual advantage of a reasonable degree of accuracy) it is the right arrangement or disposition of the various values of light and dark that is particularly essential. It is easy to get objects "out of value" with their surroundings even though they seem good individually.

What we do wish to impress on the reader at this time is that if one learns early to express individual values, ranging from the lightest to the darkest, in various techniques indicative of many materials or surfaces, he will later make use of this knowledge almost unconsciously, which will keep his mind free to cope with other difficulties of drawing and composition.

As a start in value practice it is often well to make several scales somewhat similar to that shown as Value Scale (A) at "1," Plate 11, or in Marginal Sketches A, B and C. In this on Plate 11 the upper rectangular space indicates the white. The black was drawn next. In the middle gray it will be noticed that the black lines are approximately the same widths as are the white spaces left between them, so this middle value is truly halfway between the black and the white. The light gray is intended to be halfway between the white and the middle gray, and the dark gray halfway between the middle gray and the black, so the whole scale gives a natural gradation from the white to the black. Unfortunately the light gray in this Value Scale (A) seems to show too sudden a change from the white; this is largely an optical effect due to the exaggerated emphasis given to the white by the strong contrast of the margin lines around it, and to the darkening tendency that the black margins have on the light gray tone. Marginal Sketch A is better in this respect, and the student would do well to copy it, allowing the tones to be adjacently disposed as indicated. In this sketch we show no pure white or black but a graded adjustment of five values from very light to very dark gray. The change in value is brought about by adding to the number of lines in each unit of tone, from the light to the dark, and by slightly widening the lines by increased pen pressure as the dark is approached. In Marginal Sketch B cross-hatch has been used to produce similar tonal results. Marginal Sketch C shows a somewhat freer type of technique employed in much the same way. To turn back to Plate 11, Sketch 3, Value Scale (B), we see that it is possible to form areas of almost any desired tone even when definite patterns or decorative effects are the means.

Once the student has made a number of these

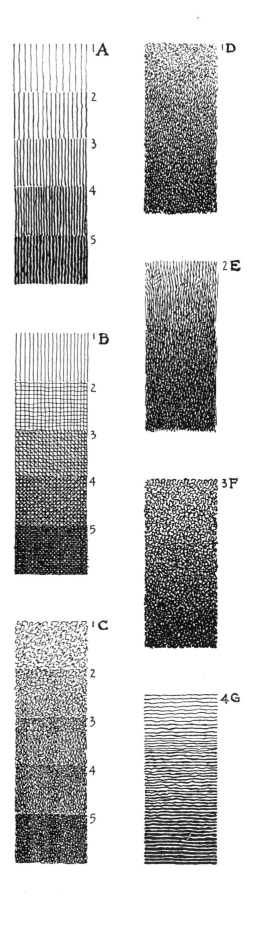

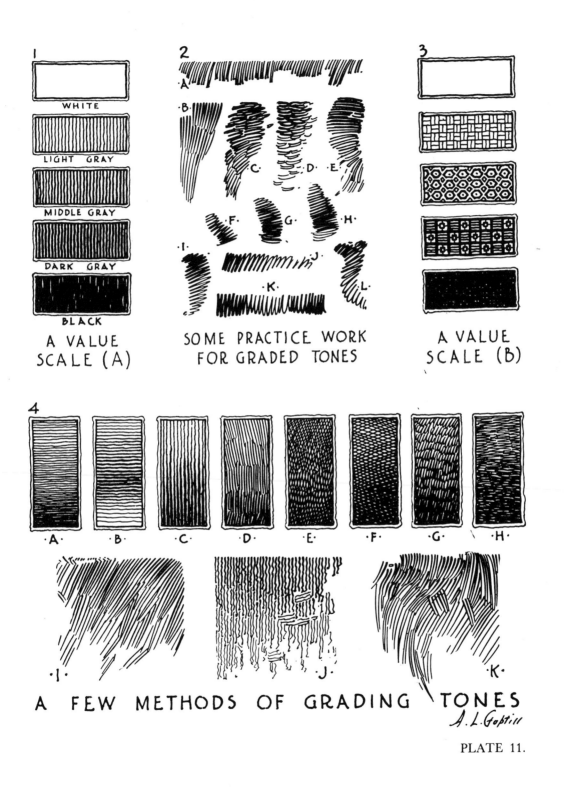

1

WHITE

LIGHT GRAY

MIDDLE GRAY

DARK GRAY

BLACK

A VALUE
SCALE (A)

2

·A·

·B·

·C· ·D· ·E·

·F· ·G· ·H·

·I· ·J·

·K· ·L·

SOME PRACTICE WORK
FOR GRADED TONES

3

A VALUE
SCALE (B)

4

·A· ·B· ·C· ·D· ·E· ·F· ·G· ·H·

·I· ·J· ·K·

A FEW METHODS OF GRADING TONES

A. L. Guptill

PLATE 11.

scales (he may add tones showing a wider range of values if he wishes, a common number being nine, or one between each pair which we have shown on Plate 11) he should try the interesting experiment of attempting to represent portions of objects of neutral color in the correct value of pen tone. He should take a bit of gray paper, for instance, and try to produce in ink, on his white drawing paper, an approximately correct effect of the value of the gray. Or he should take a white cardboard box and attempt to build a gray corresponding to the white of some portion of the box as it appears grayed by shade or shadow. (The intent should not be to draw the box, but merely to indicate a small area of its tone.)

In thus dealing with grays whose relative values are perceived without great difficulty, the problem is mainly one of representing those values. When objects are in color, however, it takes some skill for the artist to perceive them correctly as well as to translate or interpret them in terms of gray. As an aid in determining the correct value of any surface, whether neutral or in color, it is helpful to compare the surface with some white object (a sheet of white paper will do nicely) which is turned to receive the maximum available light. It will be found that many objects of different colors may have the same value, while objects actually the same in both color and value may vary greatly in apparent value, due to differences in their lighting.

Up to this point in our pen practice we have considered mainly such units of tone as are comparatively flat, or uniformly gray, throughout. These are the ones which should be practiced first, but as many objects show gradations of tone one is hardly qualified to attempt to render them until he has become somewhat proficient in grading areas of his paper surface with pen tone. It is advisable for one to try building graded tones as soon as he has acquired reasonable skill in handling the flat ones.

It will be seen that such a group of flat tones as we have in Marginal Sketch A gives something of a graded effect—if arranged as they are here—but the gradation is lacking in smoothness. It is only a step from this, however, to the making of similar graded tones such as Marginal Sketches D, E, F and G. Practice the formation of tones of this kind. Plate 11 shows other methods of grading work. At "2" there are a number of free stroke combinations running from light to dark or from dark to light, and the student should try many arrangements of this sort. At "4" we have from "A" to "H" a group of more carefully constructed tones, each of which is graded to some extent. In that at "A," lines of uniform width have been used but have been more closely spaced towards the bottom, until finally they touch and merge into practically solid black. At "B" the pen pressure has been so varied as gradually to increase and then decrease the weight of the strokes—shading the tone from light to dark and back again. At "C" we have an example of the sort of tone which is produced when tapering lines of the kind shown at "J," Plate 2, are used in juxtaposition. Tones "D," "E," "F," "G," and "H," speak for themselves. At "I," "J," and "K," are larger areas, graded with somewhat more freedom. Innumerable combinations similar to these are possible, and some of them should be tried by the student, who should have, after this practice, sufficient dexterity to enable him to proceed rapidly with the problems to follow, problems which undoubtedly will prove more interesting than any of these highly important, but somewhat irksome, preparatory exercises.

JOSEPH CLEMENT COLL

LIGHT AND SHADE

THERE ARE FEW PRINCIPLES of light and shade that can be easily imparted to the student by a text book or an instructor. Instead he must learn mainly through his own observation and thoughtful analysis. Here we can only urge him to observe and to think, and point the way for the observation and thought.

There are those who seem surprised when one mentions that the artist must observe and think; they apparently take it for granted that he draws instinctively, and is incapable of any deep thought or real common sense. Yet all drawing is much more a matter of reason than is generally supposed, and artists are usually thinkers of the keenest sort. In fact many individuals have become artists mainly through their power to observe thoughtfully how things really do look and to figure out by logical methods why they appear as they do, and by equally logical methods

59

how to suggest such appearances on paper. Anyone who can shake himself free from preconceived notions of the appearance of some object, and who can analyze its appearance in an unbiased manner, has gone a long way towards learning to draw that object, and similar objects as well.

It seems needless to repeat that the principles governing the appearance of both large and small objects are identical. If one studies small objects, stripped bare of confusing detail, and learns how they appear and why, he finds out much concerning the appearance of other things, regardless of size. Through careful observation of a simple wooden cube, for instance, and analysis of its light and shade (as well as its perspective appearance and other facts not connected with our present thought) one can learn almost unconsciously principles which apply to the drawing of the largest building as well as to the cube itself. In the same way, if one studies a small sphere (such as a light colored rubber ball), facts are learned of value in drawing any spherical or similar form—the human head, for instance, or a round tree, or the dome of a building. It is for this reason that it is possible for the beginner to profit so greatly from the study of such simple objects as cubes and spheres, or still life like that discussed in the next chapter.

The art supply houses sell sets of wooden models including spheres, ellipsoids, ovoids, cylinders and other rounded forms, as well as flat-sided solids like the cube, pyramid and prism. These are excellent subjects for observation and early sketching, though, as we have just said, still life objects found in daily use, such as small boxes, dishes and the like, also afford splendid practice for the beginner, particularly when they have little strong color or detail.

The best way for the student to learn to observe and analyze light and shade is obviously through practice in observation and analysis. The natural way is for him to take some one simple object at a time, such as one of these just mentioned, and to hold it exposed to light coming from a single direct source (as at a window), studying it earnestly, with the mind as free as possible from any preconception of its appearance. When one has selected the object (let us assume that a sphere has been chosen) and has put himself at ease where the light is good and where he can muse undisturbed, his soliloquy might run somewhat like this. "Why, here is a round white ball. How do I know its shape and color, judging by the sense of sight? If it were pitch dark here I could not see it at all and hence would know nothing about its appearance, unless through memory of it. If there were just a little light I might know little about it. But the sun is shining and I can see it plainly. I know it to be white because that part of it which is turned directly towards the sun shows absence of color. If I turn it to a new position this is still true. The parts which are turned somewhat away from the direct rays of light do not appear white; they seem gray. As a rule, the more directly the rays hit the surface the lighter it appears. If there were several suns in different positions shining on the ball it might all look white. If thus equally illuminated from every direction, it would look flat, like a disk. But there is only one sun, and the more the surface turns away from the sun the darker it seems to get. Does it? Right here at the back edge, opposite the spot where the rays hit the most directly, it seems a bit lighter again. I wonder why that is? It is because the sun is shining also on that light sheet of paper below the ball, which, in turn, is reflecting light back onto it. The paper is similar to another but much weaker sun. How do I know the ball is round? Because I see it as a circular form silhouetted against the background. Why? Because it is lighter than the background, which is not well illuminated. It is light and the background is dark, so it shows by contrast. If the background were all equally white and the ball uniformly illuminated from every side the latter might not be visible at all. The light comes from the left because the sun happens to be on the left; the right side appears gray because it is in shade. The shade takes a form that is so rounded and so graded it is plain to me that the surface of the ball which is towards me is not only round in contour but is raised in hemispherical convexity. If the sunlight were less bright the ball would seem darker; if there were no light the ball would be invisible."

This undoubtedly sounds rather simple, and it is true that these rambling thoughts regarding the ball mean little in themselves, but the whole paragraph is most important in pointing out the general way in which one's thoughts should be directed when some object is under observation. Many artists consciously analyze each subject in a manner somewhat similar to this before starting to draw; others as the drawing progresses. Usually, however, except in the case of the beginner, the artist is hardly conscious that he is thinking at all. But unless he does think or has thought deeply at some previous time concerning a similar subject, his drawing is certain to show it; probably the drawing will not convey its message convincingly. Some artists and students, instead of drawing honestly, according to what they observe or have observed, simply perform a series of borrowed tricks of technique. Other and greater artists may use the very same tricks, perhaps, but if so they apply them with a knowledge gained through observation, which makes their work more true and virile.

One does not study in this way for long before he arrives at some very interesting conclusions. One of these is that, as a rule, the worker in almost any linear medium, including pen and ink, practically reverses nature's processes so far as light and shade are concerned. In nature, things are not visible at all until there is light; then the light shines on certain surfaces which are turned toward it and makes them visible. Reflected light makes other surfaces visible but less brilliant than those directly illuminated. The amount of brilliancy of each surface depends largely on how it is turned in reference to the sources of direct and reflected illumination. The shade and shadow parts are simply those which are not so turned as to receive the rays of light directly. To repeat, nature starts with dark and adds illumination until her effects of brilliancy are gained, and the shade and shadow remain much as they were, though somewhat lighter through reflection of light. In pen drawing the artist usually does the reverse, even when naturalistic effects are sought; he starts with the white paper and allows that to represent the most brilliantly lighted surfaces; then with the pen he applies the shade and shadows. In other words, he puts darks on such areas of his drawings as

EDWARD BAWDEN

represent shade and shadow, leaving the white paper to represent the lights; but nature does the opposite, she puts on lights or illuminates the objects themselves in the areas turned toward the source of illumination, leaving the remainder in almost its original darkness. The effect is much the same; the method contrary. If the student fully comprehends this reversal, all his work will be more intelligently handled from the start.

The reader is now referred to Plate 12. In the sketches at "1," "2" and "3," a sphere has been drawn in pencil. In the first sketch, that at "1," the light is coming downward from the left, as indicated by the arrow. Where the light falls most directly on the curved surface there is an area of high light—the most brilliant spot on the entire sphere. From this spot the spherical surface gradually darkens in every direction, and particularly in that opposite the source of light. As shown here, however, the darkest spot is not at the exact edge, for that is quite bright because of reflection of light from some unknown source which is below and towards the right, the brightest area of reflected light being almost opposite the brightest spot of direct light. In the sketch at "2," the source of light is no longer at the left but in front of and above the sphere, and so the light shines downward. This causes the area of high light to move towards the center, near the top, and the darkest dark to move towards the bottom, as indicated. The area of reflected light also moves towards the bottom, and, though the location of such a tone is always dependent on the position of the surface from which the light is reflected, here, as is generally customary, it shows directly below the darkest dark. In "3" the source of light is again differently located, the rays falling upon the sphere from a source in front and to the right. This brings the area of highlight towards the right, the darkest dark and brightest reflected area towards the left.

In the case of the three rounded forms at "4," "5" and "6," the light is coming from a source similarly located to that in "1," as shown both on the plans and the perspectives. Note that the ovoid form at "4" is almost like the spherical solid above it at "1" in its general disposition of light and shade. In the case of the cylinder at "5," and the cone at "6," the high light is also towards the left and the reflected light towards the right, with the darkest dark near the reflected light. These reflections as shown on this plate, though no brighter than such tones often are, are rather extreme; reflections should usually be sacrificed by darkening a bit; they were made too prominent here in order to make their locations plain.

One should not assume from these sketches that such forms are always lighted from these directions, for obviously this could not be so; neither should it be thought that reflected light is always present, for without something to cause it it could not be. These are the most common directions of lighting, however, and as reflections are often evident the student must be well acquainted with them.

The reader should now turn to sketches "7," "8" and "9." These flat-sided solids take the same general shapes as do "4," "5," and "6," respectively. Under the same lighting, however, it will be noted that they appear quite different. First, most of their profiles seem more angular and pointed. Second, the light and shade is now broken up into flat planes, instead of being graded as in the rounded solids above.

We go to considerable pains here to explain some of the various differences in appearances as seen in a few small and easily understood objects, mainly in order to teach the student to analyze all subjects in this way, not only these and other simple geometric shapes, but also such forms as are discussed in the next chapters.

1 · SOURCE OF LIGHT
HIGH LIGHT
REFLECTED LIGHT

2 · SOURCE OF LIGHT
DARKEST DARK
REFLECTED LIGHT

3 SOURCE OF LIGHT
REFLECTED LIGHT
HIGH LIGHT

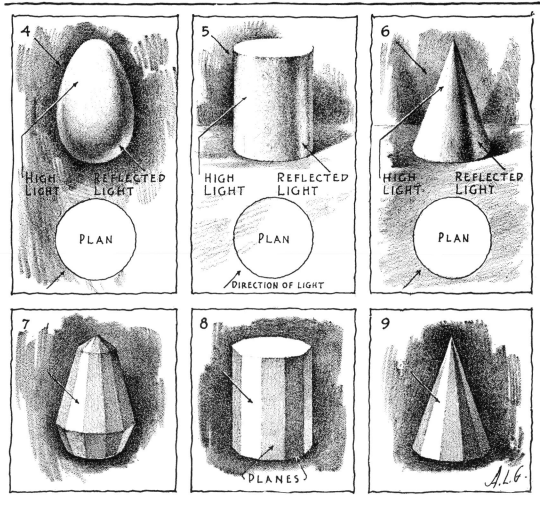

4
HIGH LIGHT
REFLECTED LIGHT
PLAN

5
HIGH LIGHT
REFLECTED LIGHT
PLAN
DIRECTION OF LIGHT

6
HIGH LIGHT
REFLECTED LIGHT
PLAN

7

8
PLANES

9
A.L.G.

PLATE 12.

EDWARD SMITH

OBJECT DRAWING IN LIGHT AND SHADE

DRAWING in light and shade is usually a welcome subject for the would-be artist. This subject is particularly welcome to the beginner who has patiently prepared himself for it, not only by working his way through many exercises in line practice and tone building (including the making of value scales) but also by conscientiously experimenting with numerous kinds of outline and applying them to a wide variety of subjects. To him light and shade work stands as a sort of reward for all this practice, a large part of which has perhaps been of so preparatory a nature as to have brought him little real pleasure in the doing. He faces light and shade not only with enthusiasm but with confidence—confidence born of this preparation yet tempered by it, for long practice brings the knowledge, as nothing else could, that perseverance is always a requisite of the pen student, and so will be as much needed in his new work as it was in the old.

It is true that a beginner sometimes omits all such study as we have discussed in the early chapters of this volume, starting his pen practice by immediately drawing in light and shade, and he sometimes does so successfully. There is little to condemn in this method, though sudden discouragement is likely to come to one who follows it, unless he already has a thorough working knowledge of some similar medium, or more than ordinary ability coupled with a persevering nature. This is particularly true if he attempts subjects which are too difficult, a thing he may feel strongly inclined to do unless forewarned, in which case he should deliberately curb his ambition and enthusiasm. The author has known beginners to try at once to draw faces or figures in pen, or street scenes or large buildings or complex landscapes, and, failing to get the desired effects, to give up the whole thing in disgust, with the feeling that they were lacking in the necessary talent; in reality their trouble was lack of judgment and perseverance rather than lack of innate ability.

So, whether one has ever done any preparatory pen work or not, he should realize that light and shade will tax both patience and skill, consequently he should start with simple subjects, such as geometric solids or still life objects.

From this simple beginning he should pass on gradually to attempt more difficult subjects, advancing only as fast as increased skill permits, thus mastering each phase of pen work in turn. There is nothing but harm in a superficial rushing on from one kind of subject and method of treatment to another. He who has had no preliminary practice must expect to make up for the lack of it as he goes along; he may find his progress a bit slower than that of the person who has first built up such a solid background as we have recommended.

Working space—Whatever subjects the beginner may select to study and draw as his first problems in light and shade representation, he will be laboring under a distinct handicap unless he is he is able to provide himself with a satisfactory place for the carrying on of his work. This should preferably be one where he can be alone and undisturbed, or where others about him are doing the same or similar exercises, as in an art school or studio. In many ways one's own home is the best place of all. The ideal arrangement is to have an entire room, or at least one end of a room, where objects can be placed or compositions arranged to the best advantage and left untouched until the drawings are completed; a place where drawing table or easel, pens and inks and other materials will remain undisturbed; above all, a place permitting proper lighting of both drawing board and objects to be drawn. A single source of light is preferable to two or more, for the more sources there are the more complicated is the light and shade. With light from a single source, for instance, the shade and shadow effects are comparatively simple, the shadow shapes themselves being quite plainly defined. With light from several sources there are often several shadows from each object, these are frequently blurred together in a most confusing way—aside from

this there are complications due to reflected light.

Our last word about the lighting of the room is perhaps the most important of all; this is that the window should face towards the north, if possible. North light, being largely reflected from the sky, is more pure in hue and more uniformly steady than is light from any other direction. This means that if one sets up a still life composition in the morning, he will find that its light and shade will remain almost constant throughout the day, an obvious advantage. It is particularly disturbing to have brilliant sunlight streaming into a room where work in light and shade is being done, for it is not only constantly changing in its own intensity and direction, but it causes additional changes through reflection from the many surfaces on which it falls. Aside from this it is dazzling and confuses one's sense of the values in the objects themselves.

So much concerning the larger pieces of essential equipment. The student should be able to find easily satisfactory positions for the pens and ink—probably to the right, if he is right handed. Many of the adjustable tables provide for these smaller accessories.

This concludes our list of special equipment for object drawing. If one is to do a great amount of this work he should also have some sort of convenient cabinet in which interesting still life, casts, and other reference material may be stored. If he plans to do little, on the other hand, he may not need the cabinet and, if he wishes, he may substitute an ordinary small table for the adjustable one described. In any case a portfolio for the storage of paper and drawings is useful, and a wastebasket handy.

Selecting the subject—When one's equipment has been gathered and arranged, the student is ready to select his first subject. This, as we have pointed out, might advantageously be very simple, consisting of a single object showing no marked texture and little contrast in color.

Analysis of subject—Once selected, the next task is to analyze the subject before starting to draw. What are its principal attributes? Is it large or small? Is it high or low? Is it round or square? Is it light or dark in tone? Is it rough or smooth? Are its edges regular or irregular? The amount of time given to this sort of analysis should depend on the subject itself and the state of progress or ability of the student. With a little practice one should learn to grasp essentials of form, color, value, texture, and the like, almost at a glance, yet some students fail to do so, and over emphasize non-essentials in their drawings.

Drawing—As soon as this analysis has been made, the student should tack his paper to the board and start to draw, determining first just where he wishes to locate his drawing on the paper. The main proportions should be blocked in with a few sweeps of the pencil, the point barely touching the paper surface. Here correct form and perspective should be the aim.

Tests—One extremely important test of the accuracy of one's work is simply to put the drawing back near the object or objects drawn, for direct comparison. The author remembers one studio where a folding music rack was placed beside each object stand, which permitted every student to set his drawings in an almost vertical position exactly where needed for ease in comparison. With your own drawing back in this way, ask yourself how correctly you have worked. Have you the heights right in relation to the widths? If you are not sure there is a valuable test to aid you.

Thumb measurement—This test is known as thumb or pencil measurement. One eye is closed and the arm is outstretched at full length towards the object, the hand grasping a pencil with the pointed end near the little finger. The pencil is held at right angles to the arm, or, more properly, at right angles to the central line of sight from the eye to the object. The unsharpened end of the pencil can then be used as a measure for comparing width and height or the length of one line with another, just as a ruler might be applied directly to the objects themselves, the end of the pencil marking one point and the thumbnail being allowed to slide along on the pencil until it marks the next desired point; the amount of pencil exposed from the uncut tip to the nail then being compared as a unit of measure with some other line or space to be measured. When it is desired to compare one line with another in length, it is best to take the smaller on the pencil first and use it as a unit of measure for the other. As the various proportions in each object are compared in this way, the corresponding proportions on the drawing may also be compared, either by the eye or by laying the pencil flat on the paper itself. If they are not relatively the same, the differences will be obvious and corrections can be made. The value of this test is lost unless, while measuring, the pencil is constantly kept at exactly the same distance from the eye. So the elbow must not be bent or the body turned; therefore keep the shoulders firm against the chair back.

At best this method of measurement is useful merely as a test, as it is only approximately accurate, so the student should not depend on it too frequently, but should, instead, rely mainly on the eye, especially for the smaller proportions. As a test, however, it is valuable, not only in object drawing, but in life drawing, nature sketching, and other types of work.

The pencil may be used in another way, too, as an aid in getting true proportion, and the slant of various lines. It may be held at arm's length in such a position that it hides, or coincides with, some important line in the object—

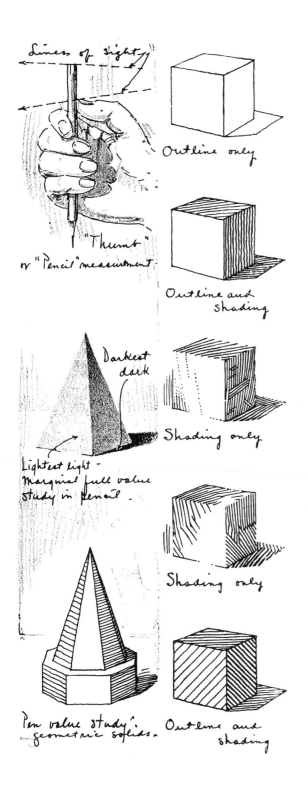

Lines of sight

"Thumb"
or "Pencil" measurement.

Outline only

Outline and shading

Darkest dark

Lightest light —
marginal full value
study in pencil.

Shading only

Shading only

Pen value study:
geometric solids.

Outline and shading

then it may be compared with the same line in the drawing. Or one may hold it vertically or horizontally and then sight across it to some sloping line, comparing slopes, and the angles formed by various intersecting edges.

Value studies—Once a subject has been blocked out in pencil, tested, and worked over until correct in form, the pencil lines should be softened by erasing until they become merely faint guides for the inking. Before the inking is done it is often advisable in a first subject, or complicated later ones, to make a study in pencil, or perhaps in pen, of the values of light and shade. This may be in the form of a little separate sketch, possibly on the margin of the paper.

Such a sketch helps one to determine, before the pen is picked up, just how dark to make his tones. Often just before the inking is begun a larger study is made in pencil on tracing paper laid over the drawing. This is an excellent method when the drawing is small, but takes almost too long when large. By whatever method a study is made, however, or at whatever size, the student should work thoughtfully. In the tones before him he should look for the lightest value. It is not always easy to tell this, or to tell how light or dark any tone is. As an aid, it is suggested that the student hold up a bit of white paper, and perhaps a piece of black paper also, for comparison with the tones of the object. How light is the lightest value in relation to the white paper? How dark is the darkest? How does the darkest value compare with the black paper? Is the shadow as dark as the black paper? When one has decided which area in the object is the lightest and which the darkest, and the relative degrees of light and dark in the others, he may represent them in his trial sketch. In doing this he should notice whether or not the various values are flat in tone or graded, and should interpret them accordingly. Likewise he should give attention to the edges of each plane of tone, whether sharp and clean-cut or blurred and indefinite. He should look for the sharpest edge of all and keep it the sharpest in his sketch. His trial sketch, then, for first subjects, whether large or small, should be as accurate an interpretation of form and of values as time permits, though with little attention given to technique or to the indication of textures.

Inking—For a few problems at this stage in the progress of the student, it is usually best to carry on the pen work in quite a naturalistic way, in accordance with the true values as laid out in the value sketch. After the first, however, the student should recall the technical limitations of the pen, remembering that values as a whole are simplified or changed in various ways, sometimes being done away with entirely, especially the lighter grays. When the student plans to make these characteristic pen drawings, which are simplified or conventionalized interpretations of his subjects, he may largely decide in his trial sketch on their strength and arrangement; then in his final pen work he should express them to the best of his ability. The disposition of the values, whether naturalistic or conventional, is most important.

Technique—Too often the student thinks so much about the kind of technique to use that he neglects his values. Technique is important, of course, yet the essential thing is to let the technique be a natural expression of the form and texture and color of the subject. We shall come back to this later.

A practical problem—We are going to assume that the student has selected as the subject for his first pen drawing in light and shade a simple wooden cube a couple of inches or so in size. We have prepared Plate 13 to illustrate some of the possibilities of its representation. The student has placed the cube near the center of the object

rest and is about to shade his trial sketch, which he has already blocked out correctly in pencil. He notes that the object stand itself, being made of white cardboard, appears very light—lighter than the wood of the cube—so he decides to let the white of his paper stand for that white background tone. He observes that the front of the cube facing him is well lighted; he represents that in pencil by very light gray. The top of the cube seems to him the next darker value, so he adds that with a darker pencil tone. The side of the cube which is turned away from the light is still darker, and this area he also correctly pencils in his sketch. Each of these three tones seems to him almost uniformly flat, so he represents them that way. The shadow tone seems the darkest of all, especially towards the front, so he grades it as it appears. He sets it back near the cube for comparison, decides it will do as a guide for the pen work, and so brings out his pens and is ready to ink.

Now up comes that question of technique again. He must decide what directions to give to his lines. In some subjects the forms or textures of the surfaces or some other definite factors determine this. Here, in the cube, the form is so simple that direction makes little difference, as is shown by the many drawings of the cube on this page.

These sketches are sufficient to show that a great variety of treatments is possible for a single subject, even when that subject has uniform color and little texture. If it had more color or greater texture, or greater variety of form, or if one turned to the use of curved lines, the satisfactory combinations would be almost inexhaustible.

Now to turn back to the student's own practice, it is by no means necessary for him to make as many drawings of a simple cube, or any one subject, as we have done here. After he has

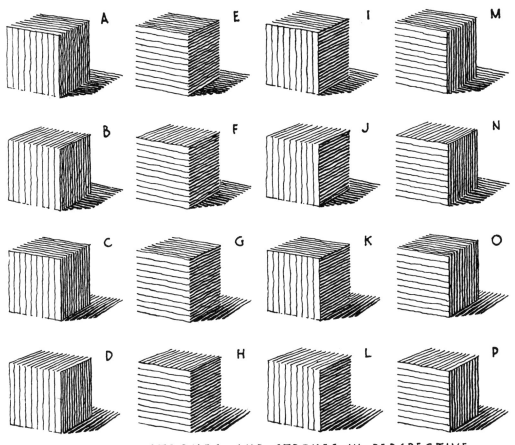

VERTICAL STROKES AND STROKES IN PERSPECTIVE
⋅ SIXTEEN DIFFERENT TREATMENTS ⋅

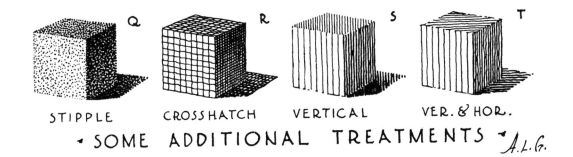

STIPPLE   CROSSHATCH   VERTICAL   VER. & HOR.

⋅ SOME ADDITIONAL TREATMENTS ⋅ A.L.G.

PLATE 13.

inked his first to the best of his ability he should make a few others, however, some with it turned in one direction, some in another, some all in tone and some based on combinations of outline and tone. Then he might substitute for the cube a simple object which, like the cube, has little color or confusing pattern. A plain cardboard or wooden box, for instance, would do very well. This should be placed in some interesting position and then drawn in what seems a natural and direct manner. The drawing need not be large; it is better to make several small ones than one large one.

When the beginner has completed a drawing or two of his first object, he should do another from a similar subject, remembering that the value arrangement and representation is more important than the actual technique. The technique should be kept simple, however, as the surfaces themselves are simple. As a general thing, too, it is well not to overwork curved lines in sketches of flat sided objects; save them, instead, for objects in which curved surfaces predominate.

Next the student should do a half-dozen more drawings, based on other simple straight line objects, such as pyramids, prisms and the like, first making trial sketches. These may be in pencil or pen. This should give him sufficient practice to prepare him for rounded shapes.

The sphere makes a good starting point in this work, as the drawing of it involves no perspective knowledge. In fact, because of the simplicity of such rounded forms when considered from the standpoint of perspective, many teachers prefer to start their beginners with this class of subject rather than the straight line objects which we have used for our first problems.

As in the case of the straight line objects, it is advisable for the student to sit and study each form for a few moments before drawing it, mak-

ing a trial sketch or two in pencil or pen for the values. We have considered the sphere in the preceding chapter, so need to say little concerning it. It is worth mentioning, though, that no matter how any particular sphere is placed on the object stand, it looks about the same from any angle, its effect changing only with different lighting.

Memory Sketches—The student does not need to spend long on these geometric objects, however, providing he works thoughtfully, before mastering them sufficiently well to allow him to proceed to more interesting objects based upon them. Before doing so, it is often helpful for him to test his powers of retention by making memory sketches of some of the forms so far completed. No instructions are necessary; it is simply a matter of trying to draw without a model, or any reference or help, that which has just been drawn with a model.

Textures—These drawings are particularly valuable for their honest suggestion of texture. Notice that the glass jug is mainly done with crisp vertical strokes; their crispness is largely the cause of the glassy effect. Compare with this the representation of an old oak bucket; here, too, the strokes are mainly crisp and vertical in direction, but they are broken, and there are tiny dots of black and white, which suggest the pitted surface of the wood. The iron hoops are drawn with lines which follow the ellipses around. The iron is shown to be generally darker than the wood, though far from black in effect. Notice the rope, in particular; the short, broken lines give a very clear impression that it is an old rope.

The basket is another interesting study of textures. Here, even though the detail is almost overworked, the general appearance of simplicity of the whole is not lost. This would be a bit hard for the beginner to lay out, however, as would the basketry on the glass jug. The old

pottery jug, on the other hand, was easier to do, and could be copied without trouble. In this, outline has been avoided, excepting in a few spots; the broken lines which suggest the corrugations of the material follow the curvature of the surface sufficiently to give an effect of roundness. This example shows strong reflected light,

separating the darkest shade on the jug from the deep shadow on the supporting table; a natural effect, for the jug, though rough, was glazed, and the projecting ridges or wrinkles reflected light as a similarly wrinkled mirror might do.

As one works from subjects such as these he

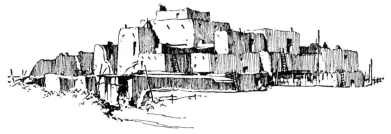

HERBERT S. KATES

comes to the realization that surface textures vary so greatly that particular study of their representation is essential. If one had a half-dozen cylinders of equal size but of different materials, they would vary surprisingly in appearance. One of natural wood, for instance, such as we have already discussed, would have a rather smooth, but dull, surface. The same cylinder, coated with varnish, would take on a shiny look. This causes us to ask why a thing looks shiny, how we know it to be shiny. If the student studies a few actual objects intently he can answer this well enough for himself; he will see that shiny objects appear so because, being glossy, they mirror reflections of light and dark, which, added to their natural colors, give a great number of sharp and strong contrasts of tone. A shiny wooden cylinder, for instance, of slightly yellowish natural hue, might reflect bright light on one side, as from a mirror, and dark on the other, the dark being a distorted image, perhaps, of some dark object. Sometimes such reflections take very definite shapes. It is common for a glazed object viewed indoors to show on its surface, in miniature, a very definite reflection of an entire window. Polished silver or other metal objects form almost as good reflectors as do looking glasses; cylinders of such materials would therefore show a wide variety of reflections. Bottles, too, are very glossy as a rule, and so they, whether cylindrical in form or not, mirror many tiny images of other objects.

This all means that if the student has such surfaces to represent he must try to suggest some of these reflections, though if he does so he must not so over-emphasize them that they detract from the effect of the surfaces themselves.

Aside from the shiny surfaces, there are many others which the artist must be able to interpret in his pen work, different kinds of cloth, for instance, and leather, and feathers and fur, and so on without end. It is advisable, then, for him to do some drawings in which special attempt is made to represent textures, and in selecting subjects for them he should naturally select those things which present real problems.

Color—Color cannot be entirely disregarded. There is little that can be said about how to represent color in pen, however, for owing to the limitations of the medium it is not possible, unless one turns to colored inks, for us to so picture an object that we can recognize its hue. Therefore color is sometimes entirely disregarded. More often it is expressed to some extent through values of light and dark; the slight variations of color in the object or objects are disregarded but the larger contrasts are made evident by tones of different value.

Four considerations, then, are most important: first, the representation of form; second, the suggestion of light and shade; third, the indications of textures; and, finally, the interpretation of color. These things should be kept in mind not only for still life objects but for every subject.

BETH KRUSH
from "Bobby and His Band"
Harcourt, Brace and Company

A FEW RUDIMENTS OF LIFE DRAWING

IF WE DRAW from any subject that is alive, the act of so doing may be properly termed life drawing. In its commonly accepted meaning, however, this term is limited in its application to the drawing of human beings from the living model; this is what we have in mind for it here. Even thus restricted it is still a rather broad term; we propose to discuss mainly the making of only those types of life drawings which are customarily done by students in the art schools from the nude or draped model, as an essential part of their training, or by artists who are seriously studying the human form in the same general way. We shall include in this discussion brief reference to the quick sketching which often accompanies such work.

Inasmuch as the pen is not as popular for most of this kind of thing as are such other mediums as pencil, charcoal and crayon, we shall be rather brief. We do not wish it thought, however, that the pen is not equally suitable, as for most purposes it is. Its lack of popularity is due more to the inability of the average student to master it than to any intrinsic fault. The pen is particularly fine for the detail demanded in some anatomical studies, and for direct and forceful action sketches.

Considering that so large a percentage of all the drawings and paintings which we see about us every day make some use of the human figure, it is easy for the art student to realize that unless he learns to draw it well he will find

FELIKS TOPOLSKI

his place in the art world considerably restricted. So the students of such subjects as sculpture, mural painting, portrait painting, illustration and commercial art need no urging to study life drawing. Students of architecture, however, and the allied arts, are often slow in perceiving the advantages to be gained from pursuing such a subject. It does, however, offer them enough of value to make its study well worth their while; this is so true that life drawing has been made a part of the prescribed curriculum of nearly every architectural school. It is not merely that the architect is sometimes called upon to draw a few figures to add interest or give scale to a drawing of some proposed building, nor is it because he may find it necessary to draw sculp-tured figures as a part of his designs, for these are relatively unimportant reasons. The study of life drawing is essential because it gives such excellent training in proportion and light and shade representation, and such fine appreciation of the subtleties of design. If one acquires the keen perception which will enable him to note and analyze and understand the slight variations between one tone and another which one finds in the human form, especially when working from the nude, his architecture will be the better for it, and if he assimilates, as he should almost unknowingly, a feeling for rhythm and balance and symmetry and other characteristics of good composition, it may be applied advantageously to his daily work. More than this, his improved

skill in draftsmanship will always be worth the effort expended to obtain it, for if one gains such dexterity as enables him to draw figures in correct proportion he will have no great trouble sketching the most complicated architecture.

Therefore the architectural student should be encouraged to take up life drawing, and the enthusiasm of the art student should not be curbed. Both classes of student should be cautioned, however, that this work should not ordinarily be attempted until proper preparation has been made or unless good instruction is available. Fortunately there are now many evening classes in the larger cities for those occupied during the daytime, and to supplement one's study numerous books are on the market.

The first thing that the student should do when he starts serious study from life is to learn to look beneath all superficialities such as tricks of technique and other mannerisms of artists. He should give his whole thought to the real appearance of the human form and to all that lies back of this appearance. He should learn how people really look as they stand or sit or walk or run, or as they smile or frown or talk or listen. As we have the chance to see many people every day this should be easy; actually it is not.

Observation—In the chapters on object drawing we spoke of the necessity of learning to observe objects correctly. As people are harder to draw than objects, the necessity for correct and thoughtful observation as a preliminary to drawing is even greater. It is not putting it too strongly to say that the primary requisite for success in life drawing is the development of keen powers of observation. The problem of representing our fellow humans would be hard enough even if they were always at rest, and with their faces immobile. They are seldom at rest for long, however, but are usually quite actively in motion, with their faces showing fre-

JOHN RICHARD FLANAGAN

quent changes of expression. As they move about, the effects of light and shade are constantly changing, too. This all makes the problem much more difficult. Therefore the artist must cultivate the habit of studying people at all times, with the thought in view of their pictorial delineation. As a man walks up the street, for instance, notice should be taken of the movement of his arms and his legs, the manner in which he carries his head, the way in which his hands are used. When a person talks, not only should the changing position of the body be noted, particularly if he accents his remarks through gesture, but the differences in his facial expression should receive great attention. Relative comparisons should be made, too, of people of different races, ages and sexes. As the student is thus learning to observe, he may be also learning to draw.

Anatomy—As a foundation for real knowledge of the appearance of the human figure, one should study enough anatomy to give him a good understanding of the structure of the body as it effects that appearance. There are many good books on artistic anatomy. In most schools anatomical lectures are given which are illustrated by sketches and charts, the skeleton, and the living model. Not only should such lectures be attended, if possible, and such books be read, but many illustrative sketches should be made of the skeleton in different positions, of the principal groups of muscles (usually from charts or casts) as they appear under varying circumstances, of numerous details, and finally of the nude figure. In these anatomical studies the student is getting down to fundamentals, so they should not be slighted. In them, for instance, he may learn the typical relative proportions of the human figure, both male and female, and many other comparative characteristics of age and sex. He may learn why people appear as they do when they stand or sit or run or walk, and why

RONALD SEARLE

it is anatomically impossible for them to appear otherwise. He may learn how even the pose of the whole figure, to say nothing of the facial muscles, may express such emotions as sadness, joy, fear or surprise. He may learn a hundred other things absolutely essential to fine work.

Studying from the model—As a logical accompaniment of the anatomical studies, and later for other purposes, many drawings are usually made from the nude model, for it is only in this way that one can get true knowledge of the human figure. The models should be varied frequently, not only as to sex but as to age and size and race. Then, too, the lighting should not always be the same.

There should also be great variety of pose. For first studies the model usually assumes a natural standing or sitting position, as this is the easiest for both model and student. Even the easiest of poses cannot be perfectly held, however, so the student must learn to work rapidly and accurately. It is here that all his previous practice will stand him in good stead. It is generally best for him not to try to work at too small a size. In his smallest drawings three inches would make a good minimum height for a standing figure, while in larger drawings two feet might be set as a maximum. There may be exceptions, however, depending on the purpose of the drawing and the predilections of the teacher or student. It is usually well, also, especially on the larger drawings, for him to keep his paper vertical, or nearly so, to permit the sweeping in of the lines with free wrist and arm movement. Once the paper is in position and the model posed, there should be a moment of quick analysis, then the drawing should be well placed on the paper with a few dots or short lines locating the extremities of the figure. A few more dots, carefully placed, should mark other salient points. Next light lines may be added, separating the whole into its larger proportions. The drawing would now seem rather meaningless to the spectator, yet if it is correct at this stage the chances are good that it will come out successfully in the end. Now is the time when it should be tested. Are the feet well located? Does the whole figure, as blocked in, show the right relationship to a vertical line? Are such points as the knees and hands and chin well placed? Do the shoulders slope as they should? Is the head of proper size? Not until the student has answered such questions as these to his satisfaction should he go on. If he has doubt on some points he should resort to thumb measurement and the other tests such as holding a pencil vertically and horizontally for comparison with some of the main lines of the model. When the proportions seem right the work can be pushed forward rapidly but thoughtfully, as large a number of the smaller subdivisions being blocked in as time permits. The main thing is not to draw as much as possible, however, but rather as well as possible. Better a figure far from finished, but right, than one pushed well along but floating in the air, or pitching over, or out of drawing. The customary pose of a half-hour or so will hardly permit more than a grasping of the main characteristics of the pose and their correct interpretation in a large way. The pen is excellent for this. It is direct; its lines cannot be easily changed. Hence one must think before each stroke is made, and try to get it right at the very first attempt.

Even in easy poses the model is almost sure to slump or move to some extent, so one should not make the mistake of trying to change his drawing from moment to moment to conform to these changes. It is possible for a model after posing for a half-hour or so to resume almost the same pose after a few minutes' rest, yet as a rule it is better for a while for one to confine his efforts to

HENRY C. PITZ

79

half-hour sketches rather than longer studies. The values of light and shade are hardly more than suggested in these first sketches. After one has acquired greater speed and accuracy in suggestion of form through outline, it is often advisable for him to do more with the shadows, spending an hour or longer on a drawing, the length of time depending on its size and character.

Action sketches—Poses showing or suggesting action are often hard for the model to take and hold, but they should be attempted, especially after the student has gained enough practice from the figure in repose to enable him to work swiftly, so that the main lines of action may be swept in while the model is still fresh. In these poses the model should be doing something in a natural way; give a boy a baseball bat, for instance, and let him put as much action into a pose as though he intended to make a home run; give an old man a wheelbarrow, or some substitute for it, and let him pretend to be trudging across a garden. Let him hold the pose a reasonable length of time, possibly ten or fifteen minutes, and then rest, resuming the same again as often as required. There is another type of pose in which the model repeats some action a great number of times, rather slowly, allowing the student to study particularly the positions the muscles assume with the varying movements. Quick sketches can be made showing these changes in a comparative manner. Boxing, fencing and the like, offer excellent movements for this type of sketch, especially if one motion is repeated over and over. Too little of this work is given in most of our schools.

The slow motion picture also has many possibilities for this sort of action work. The well equipped art school should have films showing models of all ages and types performing a wide variety of motions. Films of animals and birds and other living things would be most useful,

too. Any selected film may be projected repeatedly. Action sketches should accompany such demonstrations.

The architectural student has less need for these action sketches, perhaps, than the art student, for the nude or draped figure as used in architecture is usually shown at rest, in order that it may take its place quietly as a part of the architecture; too much motion would be disturbing to most designs. In posing the model for him, then, horizontal and vertical lines should be predominant, and the whole figure should express a quiet strength and solidity. This is the very thing that the art student, on the other hand, must usually try to avoid; if one works too long from the figure posed at rest he may acquire the habit of always drawing it that way. Illustrators, especially, must use care to suggest that their people have just come from somewhere or are going somewhere or are otherwise really doing things. They must, with few exceptions, appear alive and alert.

Memory sketches—Just as in object or cast drawing, many memory sketches should be made, with no reference to other drawings or to the model. One's success, or lack of it, in his memory sketches will help him to determine how much life drawing he needs. Much will depend, too, on the kind of art work which he plans to pursue. Some artists always draw from models; some seldom do, but depend on their well trained memories.

The draped figure—Either along with his work from the nude, or at about the same time, one should seriously commence to draw from the draped model. It is easy when representing folds of drapery to lose the partially hidden proportions under it. For this reason, when one does work from the costumed figure it is often best for him to first sketch the figure as though it were undraped, adding the drapery later. In fact in all work where people are drawn or painted it is necessary for the artist to think of the forms beneath the clothing. Work on the clothing itself cannot make up for faulty construction.

In working from the figure in full costume new difficulties are encountered, for the expression of the forms and textures of the various fabrics is not easy. But work from the costumed figure is very interesting, especially if the model is posed to tell some story. Students in illustration should do a great deal of sketching in which the problems are made as real as possible, illustrating incidents in actual life or characters in literature or the drama, the model being so dressed and posed as to express the idea to the best advantage. Appropriate backgrounds may be added from the imagination or from actual places or even from photographs.

Such work as this, done carefully under instruction, with attention to technique, should be supplemented by quick outside sketching. One should draw the members of his own family, for instance, or his friends, or people passing in the street. If they are caught unawares the sketches will be all the more interesting. It is well to have some sketch book for this kind of practice, as it is not necessary to have the sketches large. When one has no materials at hand or no opportunity to draw, he should study the people he sees about him, and imagine he is drawing them; to do this is much more helpful than would be supposed. He should try to analyze the various types he sees, too, and should attempt to store up mental images of them to help him later.

Of all these various methods of study it is hard to say which is more important. One supplements the other, and for the student who hopes to go far all are needed. Only a competent teacher can judge the needs of any individual, or can help him to meet them.

ALBERT GOLD

ALBERT GOLD

SKETCHING

ONE USUALLY goes sketching in response
to an inward urge to get out-of-doors. Spring is
in the air, perhaps, and one suddenly finds himself tired of the tasks which daily confront him—
he decides to break free from restraint for a
while, so gathers materials hastily and goes forth
joyously to play hookey.

But sketching need not be just a warm weather
affair. All the seasons, all the effects of light, all
the aspects of nature are the artist's hunting
ground. Some artists are intent enough in their
search for experience to brave low temperatures
and inclement weather, but even the less hardy
can find an interesting window view or ma-
neuver a car into a favorable spot.

The ink techniques are excellent for sketching
because they encourage a positive mood. Since
the mark of the inked pen or brush is definite
and not easily changed, it impels the artist to
think as he draws, to make clean-cut decisions

and to face his mistakes. Of all the techniques it is the most pronounced enemy of indecision.

It is not difficult to carry a tightly corked bottle of ink in one's pocket, as well as a pen and brush, or several, with a bit of stiff paper wrapped around the points and held with a rubber band. But even more convenient are the various types of fountain pens. These can be used with the usual fountain pen inks. Waterproof India inks should not be used, for their varnish content will clog the ordinary fountain pens. There are, however, a number of drawing fountain pens on the market which will use drawing inks, but even these should be cleaned with hot water or a solvent regularly. One of the best fountain pens for sketching is the Osmoroid, which has a variety of tips, the Music tip being quite flexible and probably the best all-around one.

A new instrument for producing ink lines has become popular in recent years, the fountain pen or brush with a felt tip. This tool is fed by a reservoir holding a special ink—an aniline dye with an oil base. The reservoir is filled from a bottle by a glass dropper. The felt tips are of various sizes and shapes but even the pointed tip will not produce as fine a line as the steel nibs.

This is a tool for broader, more painter-like effects. The amount of ink (on those types equipped with a valve) is controlled by the pressure used, so grayed strokes are possible as well as rich darks. Well known makes are the Flo-master, Speedry Magic Marker and Marsh Pen.

Aside from ink and pen or brush almost nothing is needed in the way of materials but paper, almost any kind that will not blot an ink line is usable. It is more convenient to have it in the form of a block or sketchbook because of the firmness of the drawing surface.

The beginner will do well to confine his attempts to something which seems comparatively easy and not too large, or if he does choose to do a large subject he should not station himself too close to it; distance will bring it completely within the range of vision, and will simplify its effect surprisingly, even though it is actually complex. Work can be done to the greatest advantage if a quiet place is selected, for it is not easy for one who is unaccustomed to it to do his best if surrounded by a curious crowd. It is bad enough for even the toughened veteran, especially if people group in front of him, obscuring the subject.

When one has decided upon his subject he should next determine from what point to draw it. Whether one picks a sunny or a shady position will depend largely on which gives the better view of the subject (a view-finder, to which we shall refer again in a moment, will help one to determine this); the temperature often has a part in the decision, too. As a rule it is better to work in shade than in sunshine, even not considering temperature, for not only is the glare from the paper less in shady spots, but one avoids the somewhat disconcerting movement of the shadows cast by the arm and hand and pen across the paper. If there are moving clouds to cause sudden changes in sunlight and shadow they will also be less troublesome if one sits in the shade, where the paper surface will not be dazzling one moment and dull the next.

When one has decided on his point of view he should make himself as comfortable as he can. If no seat is available one must stand, of course, but a few attempts to draw standing for any great length of time will usually be enough to cause one to seek comfortable positions for his next subjects.

A view-finder is often very useful in enabling one to find a focal point in all the confusing amount of surrounding material. This is simply a piece of heavy paper or cardboard, postcard size or so, with a small rectangular opening through which one may peek while searching for a subject offering pleasing possibilities, employing it much as the photographer does the view-finder on his camera. In fact the camera view-finder itself is good for this purpose, too. Not only is the cardboard view-finder useful in locating a subject, but as one starts to draw he can employ it to advantage, for if he holds it vertically and sights through it or across it he can judge the correct pitch of any slanting line, such as the slope of a roof or a line converging in perspective. By comparing the various values in the subject with the paper of the finder, a clear idea of the relative importance of each may also be gained. The student who is interested

in composition should carry a little finder with him all the time and use it frequently, even when he has no intention of drawing. This will not only help him to learn to select good subjects, but will also cause him to realize how many interesting compositions may be discovered in what often seems a barren neighborhood.

When it comes to blocking in a subject, it is usually best to work directly with the pen. One may either sketch a few of the main lines of boundary and subdivision, or he may touch his pen lightly here and there to dot off the salient points. Working directly in this way one learns to draw quickly and accurately. As soon as the main proportions are fixed and before rendering, the direction of light should be noted, for it is important if one goes beyond the outline stage, that this be suggested with consistency. The larger shadow shapes should all be located at the same time as they will change in the subject itself very rapidly.

The entire subject, including its values, should be simplified, non-essentials to the main thought being omitted or suppressed. If telephone wires or things of that sort bring confusing lines into the subject, they should by all means be left out. If, contrarily, they contribute in any way towards the intended purpose of the sketch they should of course be retained. No one but a teacher can help the beginner in making such decisions as this.

In giving the above suggestions, the usual form of rather quick sketch has been in mind— the kind finished at one sitting while the inspiration lasts. In fact, many sketches are of necessity made in that way as there is often less than a half-hour and occasionally only a moment or two of supreme interest, when the subject is revealed at its very best. Sometimes, however, carefully finished drawings must be made from

EARL THALLANDER

outdoor subjects, and in cases like this it is frequently well for one to go at things more deliberately. To gain the best results in this type of work one should first visit and study his subject a number of times from different angles and at different hours of the day, for there is an ideal time and place for the drawing of almost every subject. Having decided on the best viewpoint and hour, one should block in all the main proportions of his sketch and should then carry the shading only so far as possible while the light and shade masses compose to the greatest advantage. Then the drawing should be laid aside until a corresponding hour the next day, when the light will be about the same. This sometimes means returning to draw from the subject on two or three occasions, so the method is not recommended for general practice. Sometimes to save part of this trouble a little trial sketch of the light and shade pattern is made at once, and

quickly, as a guide for the carrying on of the work, which may then be pushed to conclusion the first day, the sketch being used as a reference for the desired appearance of the shadows. If the light permits it, and the time is too short to allow the completion of a sketch at once, it is sometimes a good scheme to take a snapshot of the subject; then the sketch can be finished later with the snapshot as a guide. The true lover of sketching will probably not do this often, yet it is mentioned as an expedient worth having in mind for occasional use. As a rule one should leave his camera at home, however, or at best use it only for catching transient effects which might otherwise be lost.

The style or method which one adopts for his work will depend largely on his subject and his purpose in sketching it. The architectural student often sketches to add to his knowledge of architecture; he cares less of what is going on in the street or wherever the subject may be than does the art student. And so it goes. So far as subjects for the architectural student are concerned, however, we should digress to add that he should not always work from architecture. If instead he selects landscape or something with which he is less familiar it will give him greater training in observation coupled with freedom in delineation—a freedom much needed by the man accustomed to the instrumental representation of straight lines and geometric curves. In the treatment of many subjects, the architectural student will doubtless fall back on outline, as he is so accustomed to its use, and there is no denying that because of its directness it may often be employed to advantage, particularly when it is essential for one to work rapidly. The landscape painter, however, is likely to do less with outline, but to make greater use of contrasting values.

As a matter of fact when one works outdoors he seldom gives much thought to method—he just draws. The method which seems the most natural and easy is, for the moment, the best. If the time is limited or if there are important facts concerning the subject which it does not seem practical to try to express through pictorial representation, supplementary notes may be written directly on the drawing.

Regardless of one's way of working, however, he should try to develop the faculty of retaining mental impressions of each subject drawn. There are many advantages in learning to do this. To mention just one, the student who can hold in his mind facts concerning the shapes of shadows as cast by objects of various forms will have a knowledge which will prove most helpful when drawing from memory or the imagination.

The devoted artist will acquire the sketching habit as part of his daily life. No elaborate preparations or long spans of time are necessary for it. Subjects are in one's room, outside the window or a few steps from the door. Any form can be drawn. And as little as five minutes can yield a few lively, significant lines and a visual impression that might last a lifetime.

HEINRICH KLEY

THE REPRESENTATION OF TREES

IT IS ONLY from outdoor sketching that one can hope to acquire a real knowledge of trees and the like. Drawing from good photographs is of course valuable training, too, and easier for the beginner; and there is no harm in studying, and occasionally copying, representations of similar subjects by other artists. As a preparation for all of this work, however, or accompanying it, one should study some of the books that are mainly devoted to a consideration of trees. There are plenty such, among which we might mention F. Schuyler Mathews' *Field Book of American Trees and Shrubs*, which is excellent, especially from the draftsman's standpoint, as it is fully illustrated with pen, crayon, and color reproductions.

A Pocket Guide to the Trees by Rutherford Platt is an excellent small paper-bound book for the pocket and *Our Trees: How to Know Them* by Arthur I. Emerson and Clarence M. Weed, is a fine, well illustrated book for quick reference. *This Green World* by Rutherford Platt is a book for arousing wonder and interest in plant life. It is filled with fine photographs and drawings.

Then there are some written entirely for the artist, such as *Drawing Trees* by Henry C. Pitz; *Outdoor Sketching* by Ernest W. Watson; and *Pencil Drawing: Step by Step* by Arthur L. Guptill, which contains a good chapter on trees; Rex Vicat Coles' *The Artistic Anatomy of Trees* is a splendid English book; although it deals with trees native to England, they are in general the same as those of our northeastern and middle Atlantic states.

A perusal of such volumes will not only familiarize one with the names and leading characteristics of the more common varieties, and train one in the laws which govern their growth, but should also strengthen the love and appreciation of beauty in nature. It is by no means necessary to learn all the scientific terms employed, or to memorize more than a few essential facts concerning each species, but it is advantageous to gain enough of a knowledge to enable one to answer such questions as the following: What are evergreen trees? What are deciduous trees? Name some of the characteristics of the Pine family—of the Maple family—of the Birch—of the Beech. Do elms grow in Ohio? Are hemlocks found in Kentucky? Name five trees that are tall and pointed. Name five that are short and widespread. Questions like these may seem unrelated to pen sketching, but they really are not. They are especially pertinent for the illustrator or the architectural delineator, either of whom may be called upon at any time to make drawings of places which he has never visited. Unless he has acquired such a knowledge, therefore, or knows where he can easily secure the information when it is needed, he is very likely to make absurd errors.

It is, of course, particularly important for one to be familiar with the trees and shrubs and grass and vines of his own vicinity, so he should visit a park or the country, sketchbook in hand, looking for actual examples to illustrate the things he has read. Before one starts to draw he should take a walk for observation. He might first concentrate on the trees. How do they appear in the distance? Can one see the individual leaves? Do the trees look flat? Do they appear round? Do the trunks seem darker or lighter than the foliage? Do the trunks and branches seem of a uniform tone? As he strolls about in this questioning way, comparing one tree with another, observing the shape of the general mass of each, analyzing, also, its skeleton of trunk, limbs, branches and twigs, he might be selecting the subject for his first sketch, using his view-finder as an aid. As a rule he will have less trouble, if a beginner, if he first draws some subject far enough from him to show little confusion of detail. A tree in full foliage is often easier to do than one which is bare.

When the subject has been selected one should search for the best viewpoint from which to draw; then he should get out his materials and make himself as comfortable as possible.

Just as for the drawing of any other type of subject, there should be a few minutes of analysis before the paper is touched. What of the shape of the tree? What of its values? Is it lighter or darker than the sky? What of its edges—are they soft or sharp and clean-cut?

Such observation will show that some trees are nearly round and much like balls—a thought which has been illustrated at "1," Plate 14. Others seem like groups of balls of varying size in combination, as at "2" in the same plate. Still others are suggestive of such geometric forms as cones, cylinders, ovoids and ellipsoids. They can be represented, then, in much the same way, yet care must be taken that they do not seem too heavy and solid when finished. And it is seldom that they hold exactly to any geometric form, unless they have been carefully trimmed. In fact even a tree which seems ball-like in general mass usually diverges sufficiently from this form to make it possible to bound it entirely with a line made up largely or wholly of straight strokes. This means that though it is helpful to think of trees as similar in form to geometric solids, they should not be rendered without also taking these variations into account.

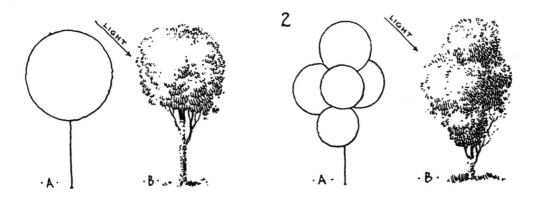

MANY TREES ARE MUCH LIKE BALLS   SOME ARE LIKE GROUPS OF BALLS

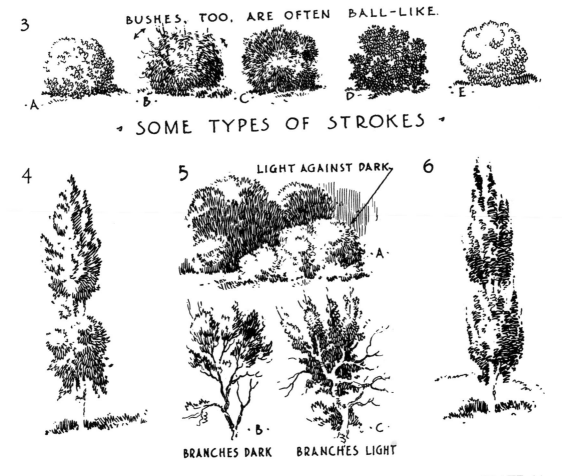

BUSHES, TOO, ARE OFTEN BALL-LIKE.

·SOME TYPES OF STROKES·

LIGHT AGAINST DARK

BRANCHES DARK   BRANCHES LIGHT

PLATE 14.

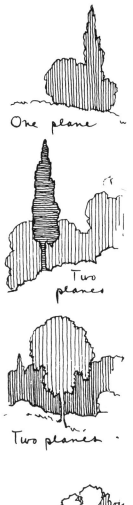

One plane

Two planes

Two planes.

Three planes.

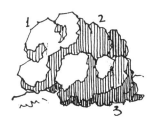

When one has analyzed his subject he should proceed with his sketch. There are several things essential to satisfactory delineation of trees, and one of them is that the outline or contour drawn for each tree should be a correct expression of its proportions. If it is, a good foundation has been laid for a creditable drawing. Unless it is, no amount of labor on the technique will make up for it. As an exemplification of the importance of contour we have made marginal sketches. These show that even a solid black silhouette drawing of a tree is surprisingly expressive of its true appearance. In these sketches, for instance, one would scarcely mistake the elm for the apple or maple.

Though we have just recommended accuracy in the delineation of tree contours, we do not mean that one has to be as painstakingly correct as when drawing portraits of people, for trees, even of one species, vary so in size and shape that the observer, in looking at a drawing of one, is not able to notice faults of proportion which would seem alarmingly conspicuous in representations of many subjects. The important thing is for the artist to learn to express the main characteristics of contour well, and especially such of these as are peculiar to each species. If this is done, one's sketch in contour will always have promise of becoming convincing when finally rendered.

As the student works at the perfecting of his contour, which is usually lightly indicated by a few dots of the pen, or by delicate pencil lines, he should also locate the main lines of growth of the supporting framework or skeleton—the trunk and the branches. Faulty construction of these lines causes many of the failures of the beginner. Therefore it is well for one to suggest carefully, in pencil, not only the larger branches which are plainly visible, but also those which are partly hidden, if a suggestion of their direc-

tions can be traced through the foliage of the tree itself.

With the contour right, and the framework correctly indicated, the values of light and dark are the next consideration. If a tree is nearby its values often seem extremely complex; each leaf which is visible has contrasts in light and shade of its own. It is in view of these complexities that we advise the beginner to draw trees that are not too near him. If a tree is in the extreme distance, and the sun is not too bright or the air too clear, it often shows only one plane of tone, which can be represented by a silhouette of gray. Sometimes a distant tree stands out as a single dark plane against another tree, or mass of trees, which appear as a lighter plane. Now and then the opposite is true. These are extreme examples, however. More often a tree, even in the distance, has at least two rather distinct planes in addition to which it is often seen in relief against a background plane of still different value. Still more often it is hard to resolve the values of a tree into less than three planes. When it comes to the final interpretation of these planes there is sometimes no definite line of demarcation left between them. The student, then, having completed his contour, and having blocked out the framework of branches, should observe the direction of light and the resulting values of light and shade on the subject which he is drawing. If they appear to be confusingly complex he may be able to see them in a more simplified form if he squints at them through partly closed eyes, thus blurring the detail. Or he may get a similar effect by walking directly away from the tree, observing it from a greater distance. He should try to think of the whole as resolved into a limited number of values, and as an aid to this it is often advantageous for him to make one or two little trial value sketches of it. Having done this he is ready to render his larger sketch.

This brings us to a consideration of the actual technique used for this work, which is a highly important matter for it is here that the student, and particularly the beginner, seems to have the greatest trouble. This is often because he tries too hard; instead of using the technique which seems to him a logical expression of that which is before him, he attempts to apply some method he has seen used by some other artist, and perhaps for an entirely different purpose. He knows, of course, that he cannot hope to render every leaf; instead he should study the general direction of growth in every part of a tree. In some trees or some parts of trees leaves are drooping—in others they are stiff and upright. It is these directions of growth that one should try to interpret, and the strokes used should be those which seem to offer a natural expression of this growth. The stroke which one might select to represent the drooping leafage of the willow, for instance, might not do at all for suggesting the bristling pine.

When the foliage is finished on the student's first sketch, he should complete the branches, if they can be seen, and the visible portions of the trunk. These should all be modelled so as to express their correct shapes; they will usually seem rounded unless in the distance. One should notice the great difference between the tone of the bark in light and in shade, a difference which is frequently even exaggerated by the artist to good advantage.

The main shadow which any tree casts on the ground must be thoughtfully handled. Often the shape of this shadow helps to give a correct impression of the shape of the tree and of the character of the ground itself. The type of line used for suggesting the shadow on the ground will depend largely on whether the ground is smooth or rough, bare or covered with grass. If

smooth and bare, horizontal strokes often seem to give the best results. If covered with close-cropped grass similar strokes may be used to advantage, but if the grass lacks the perfect smoothness of a newly mowed and well kept lawn, strokes done with greater freedom and generally in more or less of a vertical direction are better.

If a tree casts a shadow on a building and this building is included in the sketch of the tree, it is important to get the shadow correct in shape, right in value, and at the same time expressive of the surfaces on which it falls.

When the student has completed his first tree sketch he should try others; having done a few drawings of individual trees, adding bits of the surroundings if he chooses, he might attempt groups of two or more trees. In such a case the shadows cast by each tree on its neighbor should be represented with care. Often when one tree or bush is partly in front of another there are very interesting contrasts of light and dark.

Though most outdoor tree sketching is done in the summer, the student will add greatly to his knowledge of trees if he gives some attention to them as they appear at different times of the year. In the autumn or winter, when the leaves have fallen from the deciduous trees, one has the best opportunity to study their skeletons. It is surprising what a variety of types exists. Some trees have a very meagre arrangement of branches. Some, instead of this barrenness have a surprising richness; there seems almost no end to the combinations of trunks, limbs, branches and twigs.

During all of this study and sketching one should try to memorize the leading characteristics of the things investigated, thus building a firm foundation for future memory work. The sketches themselves should be preserved, too, for no matter how imperfect or incomplete they

HENRY C. PITZ

may seem when made, they may later prove of inestimable value for reference.

The architectural student should make many studies for he must early learn how to represent trees, bushes, grass, and the like, as part of the setting for his buildings. In fact, this is important for almost anyone who is learning to draw. Trees used as part of an architectural setting are generally of the common kinds and rendered in a somewhat conventional manner so they will not detract from the architecture. Such trees are less interesting, however, than those that are unusual in character. Old, gnarled, wind-blown veterans, for example, that have fought the elements for years, are the kind which bring joy to any lover of sketching; when one has arrived at a reasonable degree of skill in the delineation of the more usual but less individual types, these are the kind he will seek.

Now for a word about trees in motion. Such trees as we have just described, especially those which have stood for years in exposed positions, frequently have become permanently deformed or crippled, either through reaching out towards the sun, or, more often, through the force of the wind. If such deformity exists in a tree the artist must try to portray it; if he cannot do so his drawing is in a measure a failure. Trees, too, are often seen waving back and forth in the breeze or temporarily bent by the force of the wind, or, again, there is simply a rustling or rippling tremor to the leaves. Such movements as these last are of course extremely difficult to suggest; however, it is interesting to try to do so now and then. The other effects of motion, and particularly the bending of a tree by the wind, being less subtle, do not offer such obstacles to the artist, who can, therefore, learn with practice to suggest them expressively.

There are smaller growing things that should be observed and drawn too—shrubs, vines, grasses, weeds and flowers. The green, growing world presents one with such a superabundance of material that a long lifetime would not suffice to cover it, but it can be explored and tasted. Bit by bit, a fine vocabulary of growing forms can be built up in the artist's memory and this can be drawn upon to build an endless series of shapes and patterns. This is not merely an accumulation of facts, it is food for the imagination.

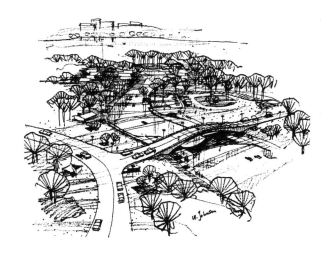

INDICATING PARTS OF BUILDINGS

THE IMPORTANCE of skill on the part of the artist to delineate architecture pleasingly and correctly is undeniable, yet it is true, also, that architectural representation is a subject which ordinarily receives far too little attention in the art schools, and sometimes even among artists themselves.

This neglect is probably due to the primary importance of other subjects, for in many drawings and paintings architecture does not come into the picture at all, and when it is shown it frequently takes a subordinate position. This subordination, however, should be no excuse for such faulty work as is frequently seen. Especially should illustrators and commercial artists strive for skill in the representation of buildings, as these are subjects which they are quite sure to be called upon to do, sooner or later.

If such work is important to them, however, to the architect and his assistants it is indispensable. For the architect not only makes many plans, elevations, sections, and details which are instrumentally drawn, thus being outside the scope of this volume, but he also does numerous freehand sketches and studies, some for his own benefit and some to make his schemes clear to his clients. Some are even done to help him to get new clients. Naturally, then, his manner of handling his architecture will of necessity be more detailed and exact than the artist would care to emulate, yet the artist would often benefit if he, too, would do enough of these complete and accurate drawings to safeguard him against the making of certain common errors, among which we might particularly mention those of linear perspective. For this subject of perspective is often a troubling one to artists who have ordinarily confined their efforts to some such work as figure drawing, where rounded forms predominate.

As this implies, a knowledge of at least the fundamental principles of freehand perspective is essential to one who hopes to draw architecture correctly. Such a book as, *How to Use Creative Perspective*, by Ernest W. Watson, would be most helpful to the student at this point. The architectural student, and those artists who wish to draw architecture in detail, should be well grounded in instrumental perspective, also, for most large perspectives of buildings are completed in a freehand manner over instrumentally constructed layouts.

This, and the next three chapters, will be treated mainly from the standpoint of the architect and the student of architecture. We shall try to show how to make detailed representations, first (in this chapter) of portions of buildings, and later of complete structures. The art student in following this through, therefore, should have in mind that to the architect the representation of architecture does not take the subordinate position that it so often does to the artist. The art student should realize, then, that though such accuracy and thoroughness as the architect requires are often commendable, the artist, as a rule, in retaining these to a reasonable degree can still render with a looseness and freedom which will convey a pleasing impression of the architecture rather than a too-detailed interpretation of it.

As a rule the easiest method of learning to render the architectural subject in its entirety is first to become familiar with ways of indicating the smaller component parts. One should learn to suggest such materials as bricks, stones, shingles, slates and clapboards—he should acquire skill in the delineation of details like chimneys, doors, windows and cornices. There can be no one correct way of doing such things, however. In the first place, a method of representation which would do for a building close at hand would not do at all, without great simplification, for a building some distance away, and a structure in the extreme distance would require even broader and simpler treatment. In the second place, if a detail such as a window is made the subject of a sketch it can be treated with more elaboration than would be advisable if it were shown as merely a part of a building the whole of which was being drawn. In turning, then, to the details which we show as illustrations to our text, one should bear in mind that they represent things close at hand, and that each, with few exceptions, has been used here as the subject for a complete sketch. Therefore the treatment in some cases is more complex than would otherwise be necessary. In every later problem where the representation of an entire building is being considered the student must realize that each detail should be so subordinated as to take its place nicely in the entire composition.

Now let us see what the student can learn concerning the indication of some of the various materials which commonly go to make up buildings. In this experimentation let him turn for help to actual buildings, to photographs and to drawings by other artists.

Stonework—Let us suppose that he decides to start with stonework as found in exterior walls. His first step, before seeking methods for its representation, is to consider some of the many effects which such walls have. He knows that walls are sometimes in sunlight and sometimes in shade, and so do not always look the same. He knows that some are nearby and some in the distance, and that this changes their appearance. He knows that some are viewed from

First cover
the desired area
with tone like
this and then

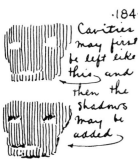

·183·

add accents such
as shadows in
the joints

·184·
Cavities
may first
be left like
this and
then the
shadows
may be
added

·185·

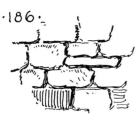

Joints are often
left white. Some
individual stones
are drawn.

·186·

Sometimes the
joints themselves
are made dark.
instead.

almost at right angles, thus appearing practically in direct elevation, while others are so turned as to be greatly foreshortened. He understands, too, that stones themselves vary in tone, individually, some being light and others dark. They vary in texture, also, from extreme smoothness to extreme roughness, the rough stones appearing darker than they are, because of their many small areas of shade and shadow. Then they vary in size, too, and in shape, and there are many ways of finishing them and laying them into walls. Some are laid just as they are picked up from the fields or brought from the quarries, for instance, with wide joints of different depths. Some, on the other hand, are carefully dressed and laid up with joints which scarcely show, giving a wall which in its smoothness appears almost like plaster. Sometimes there is no mortar at all in the joints, sometimes it fully fills the joints, and sometimes it is raked out to a considerable depth. Or the joints may be "struck" in any one of a number of ways, with special tools made for the purpose. The mortar itself may be lighter or darker than the stones.

Though this is far from being a description of all the types of walls, it serves its purpose in making clear that there can be no single way of representing such varied effects. The important thing to keep in mind, however, is that it is generally not the method of drawing each individual stone that counts, especially when large areas are considered, but rather the effect of the entire wall. In working for this effect it is seldom necessary to draw all the stones; often a few patches here and there are sufficient to convey the desired impression. If the scale is large, however, more detail is needed.

Brickwork—Much that we have said concerning the representation of stonework applies to brickwork also. The main difference is in the

Some joints light;
some dark

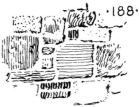

·188·

Variety in texture
and value.

·189·

Some stone
is highly modelled.

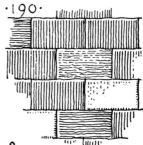

·190·

Some is smooth.
or nearly so.
(note light at top
and left)

·191·

Cross hatch
added to completed
stones.

Architectural rendering by SCHELL LEWIS

smallness of the units in the latter and the greater regularity of their spacing. There are, too, various bonds used in brickwork, such as the Dutch and Flemish.

The average brick shows on its face a rectangle about two inches high and eight inches long, which means that it is not practical to draw all of the bricks on any large wall surface. Usually, then, some effective method of indication is adopted, and often a simple one.

It is frequently advisable to vary the method of indication in different parts of the same drawing, in order to avoid monotony. In some drawings of a rather formal type a direct and highly conventional style of suggestion which better harmonizes with the character of the whole

should be selected. As a particularly fine example of brick representation the reader is referred to the drawing by Schell Lewis on this page. In this drawing not only is there great variety in the way in which the individual bricks are treated in different places (note particularly the wall by the sidewalk), but the entire tone of the brickwork as a whole is handled very skilfully. Though practically all of the brick areas have been filled with lines the lines themselves vary in weight, spacing, and character in such a way that the tones formed by them contribute very nicely to the fine effect of the values of the whole composition. See how light the end of the house has been kept, for instance, in comparison with the front. Note, too, that the front wall starts rather dark at the top and grades down to light as it (together with the light bushes) goes behind the dark fence and its accompanying dark bushes. By this carefully arranged contrast a splendid sense of depth and detachment has been secured.

Stucco or concrete—There is nothing in the way of wall surfaces easier to suggest in pen than those of smooth plaster or concrete. Often a little stippling or a few groups of sketchy short strokes here and there are all that is needed. The white paper itself generally does for the representation of the light surfaces. In shade almost any simple arrangement of strokes is good. It is perhaps better for one not to draw them horizontally, however, for if he does they may be taken for brick courses. Vertical lines are good.

Clapboards—These are also easy to draw. Usually nothing is needed but a line of shadow under each one. Sometimes, especially if the clapboards are above the eye and the drawing large in scale, a double line is used. If such lines are too conspicuous, however, as they sometimes are, particularly in the sunlit areas, dots may be substituted for part of these lines. Many times the shadows cast on the clapboards by a shutter, the door or window trim, a corner board or some such feature, help to express the surfaces on which they fall.

Shingles—In representing shingles on walls almost the same indications will do as for clapboards (and this is true, also, for the typical kinds of drop and novelty siding). A few vertical lines will add to their character. Naturally all these details should be so shown as to appear at about the proper scale, with the right exposure to the weather.

Roof indications—When shingles and other similar materials such as tiles and slates appear on roofs, their representation is most important, yet it is hard to give anything approaching definite instructions. This is mainly because roof planes as a rule are so much foreshortened in appearance, especially when viewed from the ground, that they vary greatly in effect. To represent here every course at its proper scale would often be out of the question, as to do so would make the roof too complicated and black in tone. The lines which are most prominently drawn usually represent the butts of the slates or shingles, and just enough of them are employed to look well and to bring the roof tone to the proper value in relation to the building as a whole—often not more than a third or half of the actual courses are indicated. The less the amount of foreshortening on the roof the more lines may be added. The lines which are drawn should suggest the materials in an interesting and a convincing way.

The treatment of cornices and eaves—We should not leave the subject of roof indication without reference to the treatment of eaves and cornices, and the shadows which are so many times cast by them, as they play a most important part in the appearance of buildings.

Inasmuch as cornices project from the walls, as a usual thing, it is necessary to try to suggest this projection. This is done partly through correct delineation of form in the outline layout, but we have in mind here more the light and shade application. Considering that roof tones are often rather dark and that cornice shadows are practically always so, generally the most natural treatment is to leave the projecting members of the cornice, such as crown mould and fascia, or gutter if there is one, light in value so as to create the contrast which is necessary for the attainment of the desired effect. Not only do cornice shadows act as an aid in bringing about this effect of projection but the shadow width gives an idea of the amount of overhang.

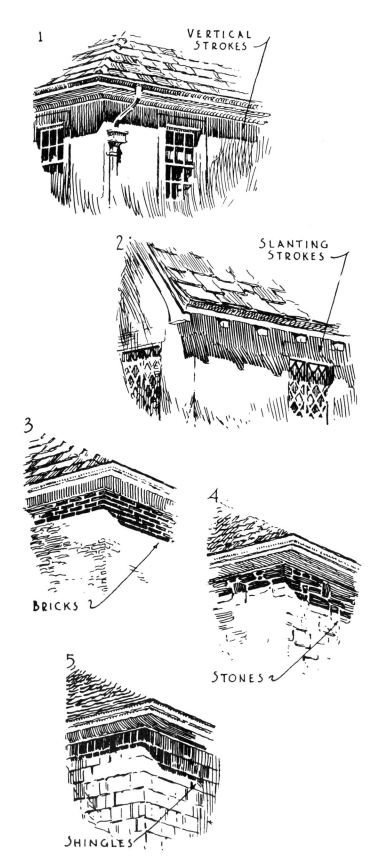

1
VERTICAL STROKES

2
SLANTING STROKES

3
BRICKS

4
STONES

5
SHINGLES

We have illustrated some of these points more fully on this page, because they are of the greatest importance. Here the cornices in all of the sketches but "6" and "7" are in perspective as seen from below; in most of them the soffits are visible, and the shadows are rather dark, especially towards the bottom. This leaving of a light soffit is a natural thing to do in many cases, for it is often true that reflected light is thrown under a cornice in this way. Sometimes the thought is even exaggerated a bit, soffits being left pure white. It is, however, no uncommon thing, as one may verify by studying actual buildings, for reflected light to be so strong as to make not only soffits light and shadows more transparent in effect but also actually to cast reversed shadows within those directly cast. The darkening of the lower edge of a shadow tone is also a natural thing to do, for a shadow when seen in contrast with a sunlit wall often seems to grade dark as it comes against it; as the white of the paper is never light enough to fully express the brilliancy of a sunlit surface, the shadow is purposely forced darker in order to make that surface itself seem all the brighter through contrast.

Shadows—We have previously had something to say about the drawing of shadows, but there are a few important points which we have not as yet touched upon. One of these concerns the values of shadows. We have already spoken of forcing or darkening the edge of a shadow tone in order to make the adjacent sunlit surfaces seem relatively brighter by contrast. What we now wish to point out is that though this is a logical thing to do and a thing which is done very often, even when the shadow is falling on a light surface such as plaster or clapboards, it is nevertheless true that ordinarily shadows vary to quite an extent in tone because of the local tones of the surfaces on which they fall. Shadows on light surfaces generally look lighter than shadows on darker surfaces, for instance. The introduction within a shadow tone of some darker areas makes the rest of the tone seem more transparent by contrast; one must be careful of his treatment however, for a dark line or spot within a shadow tone will often appear more conspicuous than one would think.

Windows—Windows or glazed doors or any objects containing large areas of glass are, on the whole, a bit more difficult to draw than most details, for glazed surfaces are so complex in light and shade and changeable in their appearance as to demand full understanding of them as well as special care and skill in their delineation. It is not hard, to be sure, for one to learn to draw a typical window or two, especially if shown at small scale, but if the scale is so large as to make any considerable amount of detail necessary it is no easy task for the beginner to do even this much well, while it is still more difficult for him to render a number of adjacent windows so as to give them the best effect in relation to one another and to the remainder of the building. If they are made too dark or too light, they may, even though good in themselves, attract more than their proper share of attention, and if all are drawn in the same way the result will probably prove monotonous; while if, instead, too much variety is shown, the breadth of effect of the whole drawing is almost sure to be destroyed. Before attempting finished renderings of windows the student should, therefore, acquaint himself through observation and study with the appearance of glass under different circumstances and conditions. It is only by so doing that he can represent it to the best advantage in any given problem. Let him walk along the street and study any windows that he sees—not only those near at hand but those in the distance as well. Let him

compare those on the sunny side with those in the shade, and those in the upper stories with those in the lower. As he makes these comparisons he should ask himself such questions as the following: What is the difference in the appearance of glass in sunlight and in shade? Do windows in the upper stories have the same general effect as those in the lower? How do windows in the distance compare with those near at hand? Can one see the curtains or shades distinctly in all the windows? How much of the interiors of the rooms does one see as he passes? Is the glass always plainly visible? Is it hard to tell if panes have been broken from a sash? Is it easy to distinguish plate glass when seen? If so, why? Do all the lights of glass in one window look the same? Does the glass usually seem lighter or darker than the sashes? Does one see images reflected in the glass? If so, are they sufficiently definite to permit one to tell trees from buildings? Does my own image appear in the windows as I pass? Are images more distinct in glass in shade than in glass in sunlight? Are reflections as clear on a rainy day as when the sun is shining?

A little observation will answer such questions as these and make it evident that ordinary window glass has two leading characteristics which relate especially to its appearance, and which are, therefore, of the greatest importance to the student. First comes its transparency. Under certain conditions glass seems practically invisible. This is especially true of clean plate glass favorably lighted. We are sometimes able then, in our representation of windows, to neglect the glazing and treat the sashes just as though the panes were non-existent, showing distinctly the shades and hangings within. The other characteristic, and the one which causes most of the trouble of the beginner, is the power that glass has to act as a reflector or mirror, giving, very often, a shiny effect to the window,

and usually images of objects as well, which in some cases are almost as distinct as the objects themselves. One of the difficulties confronting the student who tries sketching directly from buildings is the complication in the effect of glass resulting from these reflections, for sometimes trees and buildings and skies and clouds and people are all pictured in the windows, showing so plainly as to prove confusing.

It is not easy for one to know what to put in and what to leave out, so considerable experience will be necessary to teach what really is essential and what should be subordinated or omitted. It is worth remembering that as a rule the two characteristics of glass which we have mentioned appear in combination: the glass seems sufficiently transparent to enable one to see through it quite easily and yet has enough reflection to give it a shiny appearance. Sometimes, however, this power to reflect neutralizes the effect of transparency to such an extent that we find it impossible to look through the panes at all. This is especially true in windows near the top of a building where the reflection of sunlight or bright sky is frequently so strong as to make the curtains within either invisible or very indistinct. Such windows, and particularly those of the upper stories of very tall buildings, often take on much the same color and tone as the sky, and if the sun itself is reflected the windows become dazzling in their brilliancy. A reflected light cloud may make the glass almost white, while a blue sky may cause a blue reflection of a value similar to that of the sky itself. If we observe the windows nearer the street level we find as a rule that most of them seem darker than those above, for in place of the sky reflections we now have those of buildings and perhaps trees. It is useful to bear in mind, then, that when rendering tall buildings the general tone of the glass, taken as a whole, may often be correctly shown lighter in the upper than in the lower stories. It is true, too, that glass within shadow, or on the shady side of a building, usually seems much lighter than we would expect, so it is by no means necessary to represent it by a dark tone simply because it is within shade or shadow. Its light appearance is generally due to the fact that it mirrors the brightness of the sky or some nearby building in sunlight.

This may all be rather confusing to the beginner; surely this last concerning tall buildings seems something of a digression to the trend of a chapter on detail representation. What we are anxious to emphasize among other things, however, is that this very complexity in the appearance of windows in different positions and under varying conditions, reacts, in a measure, to the artist's advantage. For although most other details of buildings, such as chimneys and steps and doors, are fixed in tone, being either light or dark, and so demanding interpretation in more or less that way, windows may be suggested in almost any value which will give the best effect to a drawing taken as a whole. If walls are dark, and light accents are needed to break the dark tone, the windows may be left light; if, contrarily, dark accents are needed in light walls the windows may be made to furnish them. If little contrast is wanted, however, windows may be drawn light in light walls or dark in dark walls.

It is not enough, then, for one to be able to do simply a few typical windows of customary values; he must learn to draw some light and some dark. He must have skill to handle some in which the characteristic of transparency which we have mentioned is prominent, some which act as reflectors, and some which combine these effects. He must know how windows look both when closed and open, in sunlight and in shadow. He should not, therefore, be content with drawing a few examples of individual windows, but should try many.

Miscellaneous details—There are, of course, materials which we have not touched upon in this chapter, including logs and slabs of wood, corrugated iron, steel and aluminum sheets, plastic panels, and many others. There are numerous kinds of roofing materials such as tiles, asphalt and asbestos shingles, tin, copper, and tar-and-gravel. Aside from such materials taken by themselves there are numerous details which we have no space to include. Not only are there larger things like porches, bay windows, and similar features, but there are also various odds and ends of similar interest. Hardware offers some fine subjects. Then we have weather vanes, shop windows, signs, water-towers, ramps, gates, a thousand and one interesting forms to draw.

Once one has gained a fair degree of skill in doing such portions of buildings as we have pictured and described in this chapter, he should be qualified to go on with the representation of complete buildings as discussed in following pages.

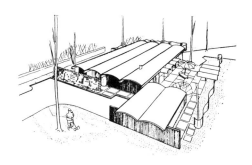

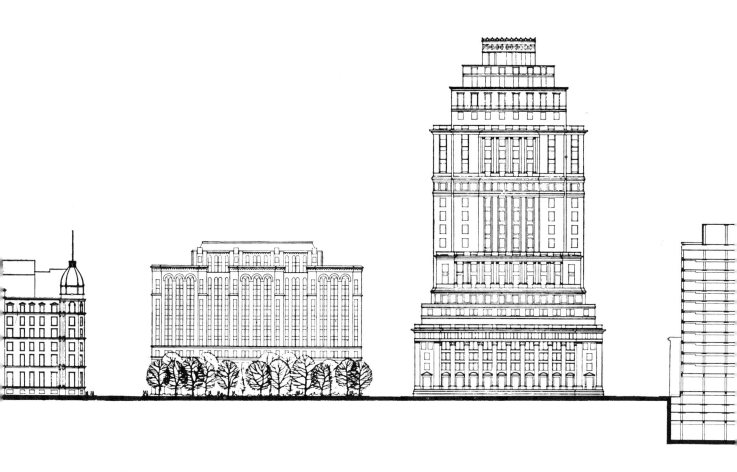

ARCHITECTURAL RENDERING METHODS

THE REPRESENTATION of such parts of buildings as doors and windows was discussed in the previous chapter. To do even such details well is no small task, as the reader who has tried them is aware. This is particularly true if one works not from nature or from photographs, but, as the architect is so often forced to do, largely from his memory of similar things aided by his imagination. Difficult as this detail representation is, however, it is generally harder still to do an entire building, where many elements must be combined into a unified whole, with each part given just the proper emphasis. Even the architect or draftsman who is trained to make passable sketches of all the component parts of a building is frequently at a loss to

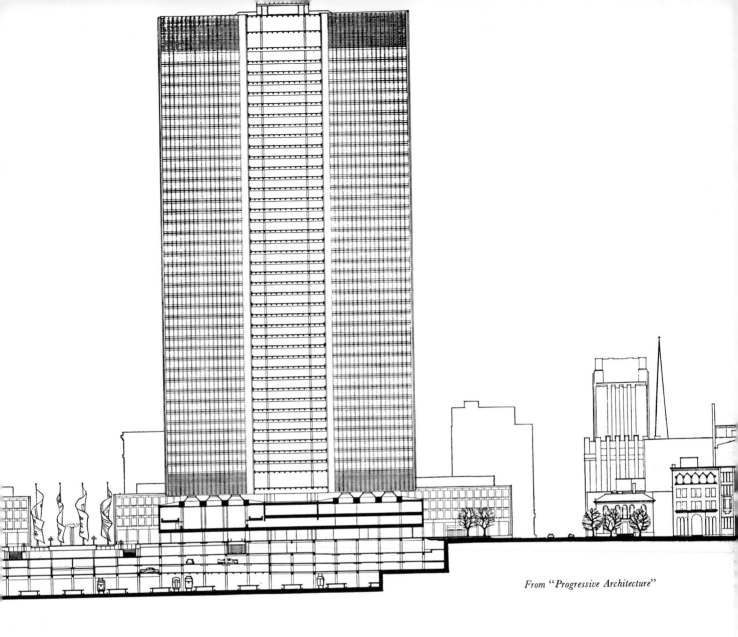

From "Progressive Architecture"

know how to start and what to do next when he faces the problem of rendering a perspective of a complete structure, especially if the setting of the building with its accessories of trees, lawns, clouds, people, and the like, is to be included.

It is our primary consideration to offer some practical suggestions, addressed mainly to the architect and his assistants (though they should prove no less useful to anyone interested in the delineation of architecture), as an aid in rendering complete buildings. These suggestions are intended to relate mainly to the making of renderings of proposed buildings—structures which do not as yet actually exist. Many of them may be utilized equally well, however, as the reader will doubtless recognize, in the drawing of similar subjects from photographs or from nature. We shall apply these suggestions, in the next two chapters, to practical problems of a typical nature.

First of all let us consider, as a starting point, a few of the reasons why drawings of this nature are made, for if we know their purpose we can judge better how to do them.

When the architect starts work on any new project of importance he usually prepares, once his client's needs are understood, a number of preliminary sketches and studies of the plans and elevations, the sections, and sometimes a few of the details of the proposed structure. Small perspectives, often very crude, are occasionally made at the same time. These first drawings are usually partly freehand and partly instrumental in character.

From these numerous studies a worthwhile scheme gradually evolves; final studies are prepared and corrected, and when approved by the client they become the basis of the actual working drawings. These consist of very accurate and comprehensive instrumental plans, elevations, sections and details. Blueprints of these working drawings, or contract drawings as they are sometimes called, together with the written specifications which accompany them, and occasionally a few additional details, are all that the contractor usually needs to guide him in the erection of the building.

The client as a rule does not fully comprehend these working drawings. They seem to him complicated and confusing. He cannot tell from them how his building will look when completed. Even the architect himself, though no doubt able to visualize the approximate final effect, is occasionally in doubt as to just how some parts of the structure will appear. Therefore, before the working drawings are finished and the contract let, it is often decided to have a fully rendered perspective made showing exactly what the completed effect of the building will be.

In a moment we shall have something definite to say about the actual drawing of this perspective. Just now we wish to make clear that if such a drawing does serve its intended purpose of clarifying the whole project, not only to the

client but to the architect himself, it is really a most important piece of work. This particular use, however, is only one of many to which such drawings are sometimes put. If a building of considerable size—an apartment house, for example—is to be erected as an investment, bonds are often issued to cover the cost. In attempting to sell such bonds it has been found that the prospective purchasers are anxious to know how the building in which they are asked to invest is to look. For this purpose, unless the building has already been erected, and it often has not, a rendered perspective of it is reproduced, usually in leaflet or booklet form, with plans and descriptive matter added; the original perspective is perhaps displayed in some prominent place. Such drawings, too, are frequently published in the magazines and newspapers, all of which is not only good salesmanship for the bond house but sometimes brings valuable publicity to the architect.

Drawings of this nature are not always rendered in pen, to be sure, though the pen is one of the most popular mediums for this kind of work, as it not only permits the necessary accuracy and completeness of delineation, but makes possible a result which reproduces inexpensively and well. Such perspectives also harmonize nicely, both in original and reproduction, with the instrumentally inked plans which often accompany them.

Ink drawing from "Progressive Architecture"

Ink drawing from "Progressive Architecture"

Now let us return to our consideration of the customary method of proceeding with the making of a typical rendered perspective drawing. Such a perspective is usually first laid out very accurately and completely by instrumental means, in exact accordance with the plans and elevations. This of course demands on the part of the draftsman laying out the perspective (he is not always the one who renders it) a thorough knowledge of the science of instrumental perspective and judgment in its practical application. He chooses a station point and an eye level which he thinks will show the subject in a natural and an advantageous way, and draws the building itself. If the site has not yet been selected the man who renders the perspective usually composes one which seems suitable. Some knowledge of landscape architecture is of great help in such work. Often the site is already in mind, however, and if surveys or photographs of it are available they help the draftsman to lay out correctly such driveways and paths, streets, or sidewalks as may exist or as are planned, as well as to locate the principal trees and other planting. They serve, also, to show what is on the adjacent lots and in the background.

This brings us now to the point where the drawing is ready to render. The paper shows a carefully pencilled preparatory outline drawing of the building, and an indication of the definitely known facts concerning the surroundings, or a suggestion for an imaginative setting. That is all. A few mistakes in the pen work and this whole thing may be ruined. This causes us to offer a word of advice. This is that in rendering one should always be deliberate and thoughtful; the pen should never be touched to the paper until there is a distinct plan for the entire treatment in mind. Too often the draftsman starts his ink work in a rather reckless and haphazard way, trusting to chance that he will pull through all right. He begins by doing the roof, if this happens to catch his attention first. He copies his treatment, perhaps, from some drawing which strikes his fancy; he borrows his windows from another, his shadows from a third, and so on. When the building itself is finished he decides that possibly a tree in back of it would help, so he puts one there, without any real reason for doing so excepting that he has seen trees similarly used in other drawings of like nature. There seems to be an empty place in the lawn so he copies a bush to take away the emptiness. With the bush in position another area looks vacant, so in goes another tree or bush or a fence or hedge. Finally he concludes that he has done enough; he calls his drawing finished.

Results obtained in this manner may chance to be good, yet it is wrong to so compose a rendering. The experienced man may, to be sure, seem to work more or less in this manner, but if so it must be realized that he has done many other drawings and so knows just about what sort of result he will obtain. And though he may be hardly conscious of it himself he doubtless has a fairly definite scheme in mind, to say nothing of the ability to carry it out. The beginner, however, will be wise to do much of his planning more definitely. Let him lay tracing paper over his instrumental layout as soon as it is completed. Next let him thoughtfully work out in pencil, observing the suggestions for composition made below, a reasonable treatment, erasing and changing as often as seems necessary. He may study drawings by others when he pleases, but should not thoughtlessly copy from them. Instead he should try to see the reasons for each thing which has been done in them. This pencil preliminary when finished will stand as a guide for the pen rendering.

In doing all this he should never lose sight of the fundamental purpose behind his drawing: that it is to express the architecture accurately and pleasingly, and honestly, rather than trickily. Whatever he draws should contribute in some way to this expression. The trees and shrubs and clouds and flowers which are common to such renderings do not exist for themselves, for instance, but only to form a setting for the architecture. This is also true of everything which enters into the composition.

With this essential fact in mind, the first thing to do, as a rule, is to decide on the direction of the light, as this decision will control the entire effect. Shall it be brought from the right or the left? If two sides of the building show, shall both be in light, or one in light and the other in shade? No one but the artist can settle this. Owing to the labor involved in covering large paper surfaces with the pen, however, and the unpleasant effect which so often results when this is done, we are inclined to advise the beginner to employ as few shade and shadow tones as possible, which usually

means keeping both sides of the building in sunshine. There are exceptions, of course, as in all things. Once a decision has been made on this point the architectural shadows should be bounded on the instrumental layout with rather definite, though not too black, pencil lines. To locate thus each correct mass is far from easy, and unfortunately even the customary knowledge of architectural shades and shadows is of little help here. Yet the shadow shapes, as we have explained elsewhere, often perform a vital function in the expression of the architecture itself, besides determining in a large measure whether or not the appearance of the composition will be pleasing. So the renderer must draw the shadows as well as he can, working thoughtfully and studying actual buildings, or photographs of buildings similarly lighted, as an aid. Fortunately for him people are seldom over-critical concerning shadow shapes, as they know little about them. Gradually one will acquire a knowledge of the typical forms as they appear with the sun or other sources of illumination in different positions. Even with this knowledge he will still use his judgment, often deliberately doing things in the way which he thinks will give the best effect even though by so doing he sometimes takes liberties with nature so far as some shadow shapes and sizes are concerned. For it is seldom that the shadows in an architectural rendering, even when done by an expert, are intended to be drawn exactly as they would be on the subject itself at any one moment; they often compose better if somewhat changed.

Once the direction of light is determined and the shadow forms are outlined, it is well to decide on the general pitch or key of values of the entire rendering. Is it to be very light, neutral gray, or rather dark? Generally it is much easier to do extremely light renderings than dark ones, and mainly for two reasons. First, a light rendering may be left largely in outline or in outline combined with simple tone. This requires few lines, and to work in few lines means that no time is wasted; also the fewer the lines the less one's chance of showing his lack of skill, as a general rule. Second, poor composition, even if it does exist, is much less conspicu-

Illustration from "Progressive Architecture"

ous in light drawings than in drawings where dark values predominate. In order to play safe, then, the beginner will do well at first to avoid dark values. A dark drawing, on the other hand or rather a drawing with strong darks in it, is usually more interesting and convincingly real and the sunlit portions, contrasting against some of the dark tones, will appear more brilliant and natural.

When one has decided on the approximate pitch or key for his drawing—whether it is to be kept almost white or gray or very dark, or whether it is to be the more usual combination of black, gray, and white—he should pause for a moment to consider what such values ordinarily represent in drawings, or, to put it differently, how they may be naturally obtained. For

it certainly is not sensible to put on meaningless areas of tone without thought of the things for which they stand.

Now values may be obtained mainly in two ways; first, through the use of the normal local color of material (expressed in tones of black, gray, and white, as the colors cannot be expressed in pen in their natural hues); second, through the employment of tones representing shade and shadow. In some drawings, to state it differently, the values represent merely the natural tones of the materials used in the objects represented; in others they indicate simply the light, the shade and the shadows—nothing more. The layman, and not infrequently the beginner, is apt to be more sensible to or conscious of these inherent tones of the materials themselves than the light and shade values. He knows that bricks are red, for instance, and he feels an inclination to draw them that way. He knows that grass is green, too, and it is sometimes contrary to his sense of the fitness of things to think of leaving it white. But red bricks, in bright sunlight, often appear more of a warm pink or orange hue, which in terms of pen and ink may be safely left light gray or even white, while the tone of grass when similarly lighted appears relatively so light that it, too, may often be ignored. The same bricks or grass in shadow, contrarily, might be correctly represented dark gray, sometimes nearly black. Now there are times when it is advisable for the student to take full advantage of the local color— now and then a complete drawing is made which depends entirely on this tone of the mate-

rials for its effect. Sometimes, on the other hand, it is enough to use only the shade and shadow tones, entirely neglecting the local tones of the materials. Most drawings are a compromise, however; the local colors are suggested in many places but ignored in others, while the tones of light and shade and shadow are also varied to meet the needs of the artist.

Knowing that we may create our values naturally in one of these two ways (which, reduced to their lowest terms become really one way, after all, this being simply a logical suggestion of the tones of the materials as they vary in appearance according to whether in bright light or not) we come to what is the most important, and probably the most difficult question of all, and that is how to compose or arrange these values. For it is not enough, as a rule, simply to give each area of the paper surface a tone which might be a reasonable representation of the thing which that particular area represents. Instead we must so adjust the entire composition that it tells its story directly and pleasingly.

Now a pen drawing, when thought of in the simplest way, is nothing but a spot on a sheet of paper. A complex spot, to be sure, being broken up into many smaller spots of varying size and force—but a spot, nevertheless. If the rendering is carried all the way to a margin line that spot as a whole takes a rather definite geometric form, within the boundaries of which there is variety of shape and tone. If no margin is used and the whole drawing is vignetted, a treatment which is more typical of pen work, the entire drawing, instead of being geometric in mass, if often simply a spot of irregular shape; within this, too, there are other smaller spots of varying value.

Spots themselves, even taken in the abstract, vary greatly in interest when considered solely from an æsthetic standpoint. Spatter ink on a sheet of paper, for example, and some of the drops will form more interesting spots than others. If a hundred such spots were collected and submitted to a jury it is probable that the jury members could easily come to an agreement on a half-dozen or so as being the most interesting in the lot.

Ink drawing
from "Progressive Architecture"

Finger prints,

another form of spot

Note the individuality in all.

Arranged.

arranged but not symmetrically.

another grouping

The row of spots on this page is rather interesting in a sense; it suggests among other things the endless variety that may be obtained by unstudied means. The next column is also interesting as showing a group of symmetrical spots. These, as the reader will at once guess, were made in an equally unstudied manner simply by spattering ink onto paper which was immediately folded and pressed flat until the drops were forced into the shapes shown.

Many of the conventional designs which we have, and occasionally renderings, particularly those of elevations, are much like these symmetrical spots in general scheme. Most architectural renderings, on the other hand, are like the less regular spots in the first row. It is seldom, however, that either a conventional design or a rendering consists of one spot only. Generally when renderings are made up of a number of spots, rather than one, the spots, instead of being arranged in some set way, like the rows just considered, are arranged according to the practical requirements of making the subject understandable and interesting. As examples to show how renderings may be reduced to a few spots we offer a few sketches. It will be noted that even these black masses, though studied to some extent in shape are no less spots than are those in the previous marginal sketches.

Let us see, now, how the student is going to profit from all this in making his tracing paper study, and eventually his final rendering. First he will try to have his entire rendering form a spot or pattern of interesting shape against the background. This will not be a black spot, of course, like these which we have considered, but it should be none the less interesting. If a subject is architectural and the building itself of irregular contour, such as one of the modern terraced skyscrapers of our large cities, its very silhouette may give all that is desired in forming a spot of major interest. A plain, blocky building, on the other hand, may form so uninteresting a spot as to seem very commonplace. If so, the addition of pleasingly-shaped clouds or trees or adjoining buildings or accessories of some sort may prove helpful in creating a pleasing form. In one's preliminary sketch, then, he should

No two forms the same except the reversed ones.

many spots suggest flowers or animals

Building renderings may be reduced to spots.

The variety is unlimited

work until he does have an interesting (though at the same time not over-complex) general mass. This can be done in soft pencil or even charcoal.

When the sketch as a whole seems to form a pleasing spot, or at least has its elements so arranged that they give promise of becoming one, thought can be given to its subdivision into smaller areas or spots, each of which has a certain amount of interest and yet at the same time contributes something to the pattern or design of the whole. The essential thing for the beginner to keep in mind is that his architecture must be expressed logically, and that he must make of his sketch a well-shaped pattern of interesting spots.

Unfortunately we can say little about how the student is to know when his mass is interesting either as a whole or in its subdivisions; if he makes several sketches and compares them he cannot fail to select the best, so if he is in doubt this is the ideal way. Sometimes the whole sketch is recomposed in doing this; sometimes, on the other hand, the various units are left exactly where they are but the values are arranged differently.

Once the selected preliminary sketch has been pushed to the point where it seems to offer possibilities for satisfactory pen work, with every essential included that is to be shown on the finished work, the actual rendering may be started. As one final test of the preliminary, however, it is advisable for the student to hold it where it will reflect in a mirror. Seen thus in a reversed position, the effect will be quite different; if it does not compose well it should be changed until it does, for as a composition it should appear equally well either way, or even upside down, for that matter. While doing the pen work it may also be of advantage to reflect the final drawing now and then in the same way as it progresses, and again when finished. Viewing a sketch through a diminishing glass is also a help many times; too often, however, a sketch looks better through such a glass than without it. Having made the best possible preliminary, one should not wander too far from it in the final.

Concerning the technique itself, we have said so much elsewhere that it seems unnecessary to repeat. We wish again to emphasize one point, however: always use the technique which seems the natural expression of the subjects drawn.

For some subjects horizontal lines may be employed with satisfaction. Now and then in outdoor subjects slant lines drawn in the direction of the rays of light give good effects, especially where shadow tones are prominent. A rainy day sketch, too, may be done very nicely with all the strokes following the direction of the rainfall. Generally speaking, however, one should avoid slanting strokes in large areas unless he wishes them to seem very restless and conspicuous.

RENDERING THE COMPLETE BUILDING

WE HAVE SPOKEN of the fact that some spots on paper, taken either singly or in groups, are much more interesting than other spots. We have explained, too, that a sketch or rendering is, in a sense, nothing but a spot, sometimes simple but more often complex, being made up of several spots grouped to form a whole. We have advised the student to try to make of each drawing which he does a spot or mass not only pleasingly shaped in itself but one nicely subdivided or broken up into other interesting and well arranged spots—well composed, in other words. We have also offered a few pointers to help him in this accomplishment. We now propose to instruct him more specifically for a few moments along much the same lines.

Mention has been made of the need, when representing architectural subjects, of so emphasizing the architecture itself that it is seen and understood quickly and easily. One of the most common ways of claiming attention or giving emphasis where wanted is through the use of contrasting values of light and dark. As in other subjects, values in architectural drawings of course represent the local colors or tones of the materials, or light and shade and shadow, or a combination of some or all of these. If we suppose that the student wishes to make a rendering of a building, his most important task, then, once his outline construction is completed, is the determination or selection and arrangement of these values. There are exceptions, of course; now and then a building is wholly represented in pure outline. Barring rather rare exceptions, however, as soon as a student or draftsman has a building drawn in ruled pencil outline ready for the rendering, his thoughts run something after this fashion, varying, of course, according to conditions: "This building is a light colored building. It has comparatively few conspicuous windows or other openings to break this light tone. It has a flat roof which from my point of view is invisible, so the building as a whole counts simply as a light mass or spot. The easiest way of rendering it, along with its surroundings, would be in outline, assuming the entire building to be in sunshine. This, however, would not attract much attention to the architecture, which is the thing that I wish to emphasize. I must get more contrast. A logical and satisfactory way might be to leave the building as a light silhouette against a dark background. This background tone might represent anything within reason—trees and grass, sky, and perhaps other buildings. To put in a complete background of tone is rather a lengthy task and my time is short; neither am I certain that I could manage it well. Even if I did, the composition might seem rather ordinary and the contrast of light against dark too obvious. Perhaps it would be better on the whole for me to darken only that part of the background where contrast seems most needed, still keeping the building light as a mass, adding outline to such portions of the building as seem to require it because they are not in relief against this background tone. I must be careful to shape the trees or whatever areas of dark I use naturally and pleasingly as they will count conspicuously as dark notes against the paper. Perhaps I had better try more than one scheme in small sketch form in order to see what arrangement would be both adequate and effective. There, I think either of these schemes might be worked up to good advantage, but I am not strong on foliage representation. Perhaps in my case it might be better to change the direction of the light so that this end of the building nearest me would be in shade; the shade tone might then give me almost all the dark needed and I could

leave the rest of the building and the trees practically in outline. Another scheme would be to draw the near end of the house in shade but to put a dark tree behind the other end so as to bring the front of the house out as a white spot against these two dark accents. If I did this, it would be better composition, I suppose, to have one of these darks predominate."

For a building as plain as this which we have just pictured, it is seldom enough to draw merely one light and one dark wall; a tree or two or some other dark tone or tones is also needed. But buildings with projections or wings often offer a sufficient variety of planes so that natural shade on some of them not only gives sufficient contrast of light and dark for the entire sketch but affords at the same time a pleasing spotting of it.

Up to this point we have been dealing with the plainest sort of light toned block-like buildings, but most buildings offer in themselves a more interesting variety of values. Windows with their shutters usually form contrasting spots, for instance, as do doors, foundation walls, chimneys, etc., while roofs, when visible, are often strong enough in opposing values to provide fine contrast with the walls. Sometimes a simple roof will do the trick of providing sufficient contrast of a major kind, though ordinarily a single dark area of this sort is too conspicuous by itself, the effect being much better if another of different size and value is added somewhere else to supplement it.

To this point we have assumed our buildings to be of some light material such as stucco or clapboards. Let us now assume, instead, that dark buildings are to be represented. A dark building is more difficult to do in one respect than a light building because a greater amount of labor is involved in suggesting a wall of bricks or any deep-toned or complex material than some lighter or plainer one. On the other hand, once a dark building is rendered the eye is often sufficiently satisfied, so far as tone is concerned, even though the surroundings are almost untouched, which means that only a few outline or light tone indications of grass and trees are needed to round out the whole. So, whereas the

Line drawing from "Progressive Architecture"

building itself frequently requires more time, the surroundings as often demand less.

Roofs may be suggested at almost any convenient value without seeming wrong or inconsistent. This is because roofs themselves actually do vary so in effect under different lighting conditions and as seen from various points of view that we all become accustomed to these diversities. If the walls of a building are light, therefore, and dark areas are needed in the drawing, the roof planes offer a natural place for one or more of them; contrarily if a building itself is shown dark the roof is frequently left rather light by way of contrast. Liberties of this nature may be taken not only with roofs, however, but with many tones. Trees, especially, may be made of almost any value from white to black to suit one's convenience. It is not uncommon to vary the tones of trees and bushes greatly even in the same drawing; this is natural, for actual trees as seen in nature do show much variation. Not only does one tree vary in value from another but the tones of a single tree are often seen to grade, for a tree is far from being a flat mass in effect. Trees are by no means alone in showing gradation of tone, however; even such things as walls and roofs, and many other surfaces which are actually flat, give a similar impression almost as often and to as great an extent as do those which are rounded. This means that the draftsman, in working for his desired contrasts to bring out his architecture to advantage, and in striving for an interesting arrangement of his lights and darks, can often fall back on gradations of tone, thus sharpening or softening his values almost at will.

When the artist renders architecture he often has a decidedly different point of view from the architect. Instead of trying to emphasize the architecture as a center of interest, for instance, or as the main subject of a sketch, he often subordinates it or in some cases suppresses it almost to the point of extinction.

Of course it is sometimes impossible for the draftsman or student when composing a drawing to take some of these liberties which we have described, such as putting trees wherever they happen to be wanted. If a definite building is

being pictured, for instance, which has existing trees about it—or will have when built—and an accurate drawing is desired, those trees cannot always be moved to meet the spotting requirements of the sketch. On the other hand, after a reasonable amount of practice, the artist or student should be able to obtain a pleasing composition for such a subject either by careful selection of his viewpoint or by his judicial adjustment of the values of these fixed accessories together with those of the building itself.

Now the student who has followed this chapter thus far should have the background to enable him to attempt to compose the simple architectural subject to quite good advantage, especially if he studies such drawings as we have introduced in these chapters as an aid. He should not forget, however, for a while at least, that time will always be saved in the end, and better results obtained, if a preliminary sketch such as we described in the last chapter is made for each problem, bearing in mind in making it as many of these various points which we have touched upon as seem applicable.

Once such a sketch is made for a rendering, thought can be fully turned to considerations of technique, which, until the preliminary sketch is finished, need scarcely be thought of at all unless in a most general way. We have already discussed technique in other chapters at such length, however, that we shall say nothing concerning it just now excepting to repeat our previous advice that the best technique, after all, is that which is directly and naturally expressive of the subject, and that of the two things, composition and technique, the former is the more important by far.

Competitions—Many times ink drawings are made to express original designs in various competitions. We are mainly concerned here, of course, with the rendering of these perspectives, yet it should not be forgotten that as a rule the perspective rendering is only a part of the entire sheet (or sheets) of drawings usually needed to make a proposed scheme clear. In most competitions not only is a perspective required but plans are asked for as well, and sometimes elevations, sections, details, interiors and even a plot plan, this last showing the relationship of the building to the grounds. Sometimes a part of these and occasionally all of them are rendered to some extent, so the contestant should try to develop skill in this direction.

Whether or not rendering is required on anything but the perspective drawing, one must always give careful attention to the composition of the entire sheet—or sheets, if more than one is required. Some able designers, however, never fully realize the importance of making each sheet as fine appearing a thing as possible. As one architect remarked, "Why bother so about the spacing of the sheet? The final building is the thing which counts; these drawings are but temporary things—a means to the end." In a sense this is true. It is equally true, however, that the judges viewing a drawing are likely to consider that good sheet spacing is almost as much an evidence of good designing ability as the making of good plans or elevations. And even though they give no conscious thought to sheet composition they are bound to be influenced by the impression given by each entire sheet, so much so that a mediocre design, well presented, is often placed higher by the judges than a better design carelessly presented. The layman, viewing a group of architectural drawings, is still more likely to select the well presented design as the best. This is often important, for the architect sometimes gets commissions from competitions where his drawings are seen in contrast with those by other architects, and not infrequently laymen either do the judging or influence it. In such a case, laymen might be blind to a good design poorly displayed but so favorably influenced by an attractive sheet of drawings as to select the author for the commission in mind, regardless of the true merits of the architecture. This condition may be unfair, but it sometimes exists and as long as it does the contestant must recognize it and try to meet it. He should work, then, not only to produce excellent designs which would actually build well but also to present his schemes as attractively as possible. Aside from these other advantages of doing so, the designer can learn practically as much concerning good design through working

for fine page arrangement and treatment as by studying on his plans and facades.

When a perspective drawing and plans and perhaps details of a building are grouped on one sheet, the perspective is really the most important thing. Frequently it is the largest single unit of all. It should be placed upon the paper, then, in a commanding position, and this usually means the top. Sometimes the designer lays it out in this position without much of a definite scheme in mind and then fits the plans and details below it as well as he can. Instead the perspective should be drawn, or at least blocked out, on another sheet of paper, tracing paper being commonly used. This sketch should be shifted to various positions on the final sheet, sketches of the plans and other required drawings being shifted in the same way at the same time, until a logical and interesting arrangement is found for all these larger units. Even the location of the necessary lettering should be carefully studied. Then the final perspective can be drawn exactly where planned, or transferred from another paper.

It may interest the reader to learn that in competitions of this nature it is not unusual for the contestant to engage the services of a professional architectural delineator to help him in his rendering or to do it for him, the delineator's name in such a case customarily remaining anonymous.

We should not leave the impression that these competition drawings or other drawings of proposed buildings are the only ones of interest or value to the architect, for it is not an uncommon thing for the architect or the student of architecture to make sketches of actual buildings. The reasons for doing this of course vary, but a point which seems worth mentioning just now is that the draftsman who wishes to learn how to render proposed buildings can do so in no more logical way than through the sketching of existing structures.

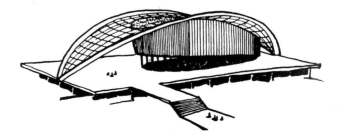

THE LARGER ARCHITECTURAL PROBLEM

FIRST OF ALL we wish to remind the reader that unless the instrumental layout for the rendering of any large structure is satisfactory the renderer works under a distinct handicap. There are architects and draftsmen—many of them—who seem to assume that if an instrumental perspective is correctly drawn that is enough; we wish to repeat our previous statement regarding the fallacy of this. It takes a degree of judgment which is usually gained only from considerable experience to select the best station point, the proper height of the horizon line, and the like. This is particularly true if a building is complicated in its masses.

In the typical perspective if one places the station point too close to a building the principal vanishing points will fall so near to each other that the perspective will be in danger of becoming unpleasantly acute. It should be remembered that unless one is back some distance from an extremely tall or wide building he cannot see the whole of it without shifting the eyes. In instrumental perspective it is assumed that the eyes are looking fixedly in one direction. It follows, therefore, that one should make sure, in laying out his instrumental work, that his station point is far enough back to correspond with an actual point from which the completed structure could be viewed as a unit when looking in one fixed direction. One well known delineator often takes this point away a distance equal to about two to two and a half times the height of any tall building, or about twice the visible width of a wide building. Another general rule is to stand away from the nearest corner of a building a distance sufficient to permit an imaginary horizontally-placed cone, with its tip at the station point and with every element of its conical surface forming an angle of thirty degrees with the horizontal line of sight from this point (or eye) to the building, to completely enclose or contain the building itself. This is based on the assumption that the eye sees things distinctly within a cone of about sixty degrees.

There is, however, no fixed rule. Until one has had considerable experience in the layout of such perspectives it is advisable to draw at small scale a trial perspective of the main lines of each structure attempted, as explained in the previous chapters. In doing this, if the station point is taken too close it will doubtless be noticed, once the main lines are drawn, that the perspective seems too sharp and unnatural—the top of a tall building will perhaps appear pointed to an acute angle at the nearer corner. This is always an unpleasant effect.

Another important point in both preliminary sketches and final drawings is that a building in angular perspective will not show to best advantage, particularly if on a corner lot, unless it is so turned that it may be viewed at unequal angles, so that one face—the principal one—is less foreshortened than the other. This not only tends towards increased unity but gives added interest; it makes a more natural effect possible, also.

The height of the eye level or horizon line on which the main vanishing points are located is important, too. In drawing small buildings this is usually assumed to be only four to six feet above the ground. So the effect gained is as though the building were viewed by a person from a normal standing position on a level site. If so low a horizon line is used for an extremely tall building, however, the result is sometimes unfortunate in the fact that the perspective of the top seems too acute, just as when the station point is taken too close to the structure. It is not

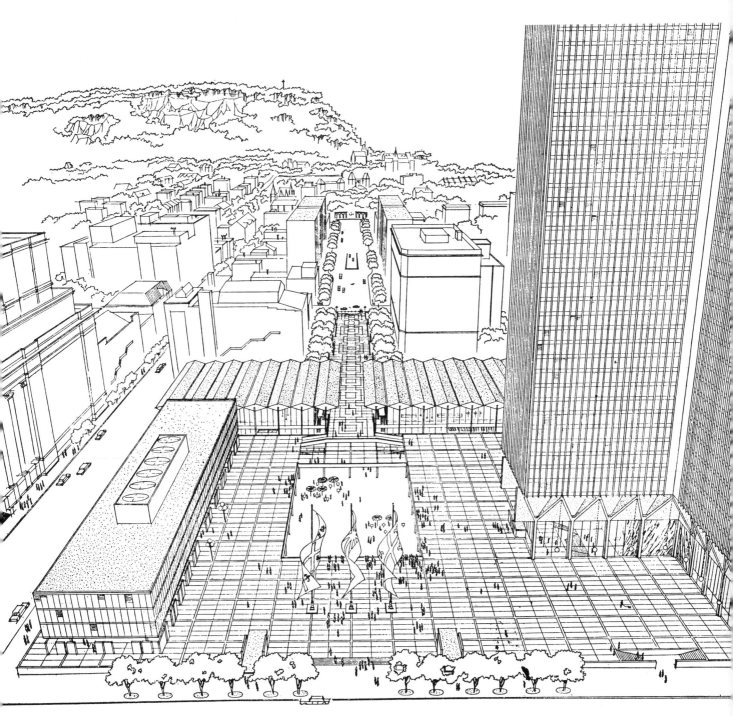

Line drawing from "Progressive Architecture"

119

uncommon, therefore, to fix the horizon line thirty or forty feet above the ground, the final drawing giving the impression that the spectator would gain if viewing the building from the third or fourth floor of some opposite structure. One delineator makes it a general rule to place his eye level at about one-fifth of the total height of his subject; another goes higher, placing it at approximately one-third. One should study various renderings with this thought in mind. It is easy to discover the horizon on each as it is at that level at which none of the horizontal lines of the structure itself appear to slant in perspective.

In making perspectives one can usually best determine his eye level, just as he can his station point location, only by making such a small trial perspective sketch as we have mentioned. This is especially essential since the recent zoning laws in New York and other cities have complicated the upper stories of large buildings, for with the typical set-backs it is necessary to get the best possible viewpoint not only in respect to distance from the building but also in relation to the ground. If the eye level is placed high it will probably result in the top stories showing to better advantage, but the sidewalks and street will be less foreshortened, and hence seem more conspicuous; the spectator will be looking down, too, on the people and the tops of the automobiles. It takes more time and skill, perhaps, to handle these accessories successfully in this position. If the eye level is extremely high the near angle of intersection of the building and sidewalk may seem too acutely distorted, one getting the impression that the building is resting on a point; this condition is further exaggerated if the station point is too close.

Once these main problems have been settled by a small trial sketch or two (which may also be used, if one wishes, for study of the values) the large perspective may be safely drawn. Then the delineator is ready to give attention to his rendering.

So far as this rendering is concerned, let us first give a word of warning against complication. We have repeatedly pointed out that one of the characteristics of excellent pen technique is simplicity, yet in spite of the fact that the student or draftsman realizes this he nevertheless often falls into doing much more than is necessary, with the result that it takes him longer than it should to do his rendering and, when it is done, the whole effect is overworked.

This does not mean that renderings of large or complicated structures can be done hurriedly —even the expert has to spend a great amount of time on them, every square inch of rendered surface requiring just about so much effort. It does mean, however, that much time can be saved, by either the novice or the professional delineator, by careful advance planning of the work. The more complex the subject the more need there is for planning.

The expert often gives little conscious effort to this preparatory planning, for experience naturally has taught him how to use his time to advantage. The beginner, however, is strongly urged to make preliminary studies not only of the sort already described but also of the values as well, first deciding on the direction of the light, as this is so important in determining the main masses of shade and shadow. He should bear in mind this matter of simplicity; he should realize, for instance, that in a tall building having many windows alike it is not essential to draw each one fully and carefully. The time should be given to gaining a satisfactory effect in the work as a whole, concentrating the effort on such details as are unusual or exceptionally important. The entrance way is so essential a part of most large buildings, for example, that it should ordinarily receive its full share of attention. Many times the best method of treating the tall building is to concentrate the attention around the entrance, the lower stories, and the nearby street and immediate surroundings, making that area the center of attention. In this case the upper stories may be slighted—a natural treatment—for when tall buildings are looked at from the customary point of view the upper stories are usually well out of the direct range of vision.

There are exceptions, of course. In a building which starts rather plainly at its base, rising gradually with increased ornateness until it is

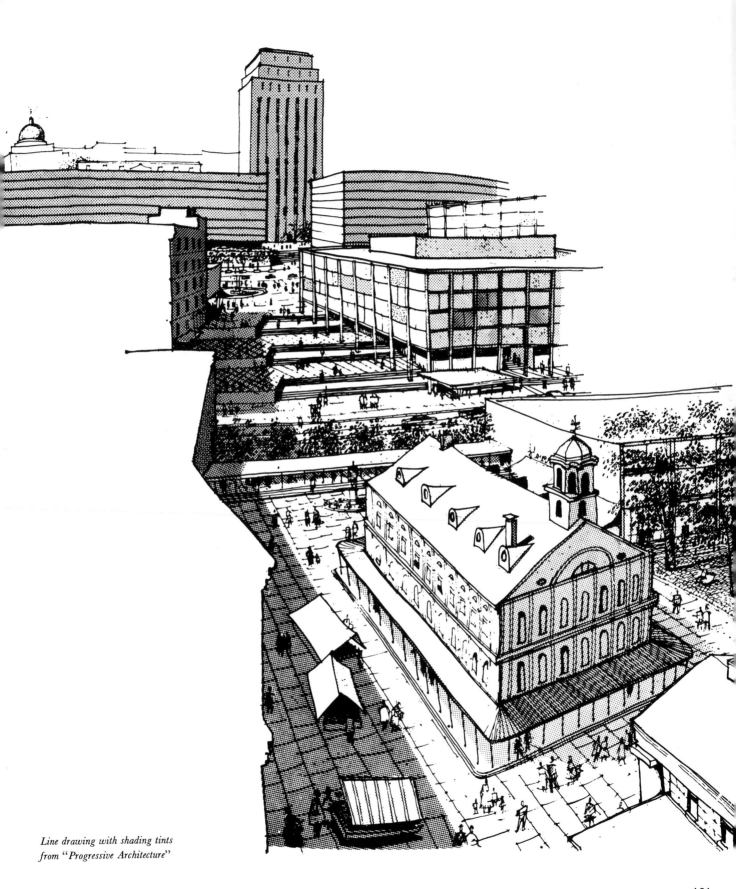

*Line drawing with shading tints
from "Progressive Architecture"*

121

Line drawing with shading tints
from "Progressive Architecture"

terminated by a beautiful tower, this tower and the portions of the structure immediately below it may logically become the focal point. In this case the base of the building should not be made too attractive or the difficulty of having two leading centers of interest, with a consequent division of attention, may be evident.

In the case of the large building and particularly the tall building, one has somewhat less opportunity, perhaps, of doing much with his accessories—especially shrubs and trees—than when dealing with smaller structures. One may, of course, show adjoining buildings. He is almost sure to need people and automobiles, too, for a drawing of a large building looks far more barren without these things than does a rendering of a smaller subject. And all of these accessories must be right in scale or the scale of the building itself will look wrong.

One must use care, also, not to scatter his figures so that each becomes too conspicuous; as a rule figures should be in pairs or groups of three or more. And we should repeat that in any such work the people must not be standing stiffly; they should be going somewhere or doing something. If the building is at a street corner, proper traffic regulations of the particular city in mind should be observed to a reasonable extent.

As a general rule a client likes to have it appear that his building is a busy place; consequently the people should in many instances be grouped near it or shown entering it. The turning of figures towards a building seems not only to add to the importance of the building but such figures serve, also, to emphasize the center of interest. Contrarily many figures moving away from a building seem to lead the attention away with them.

It is often the case that a dark tone at the base of the drawing of a tall building helps to steady the whole drawing. Sometimes this tone simply represents the natural values of the street with its figures and the like. Frequently, however, it is a shadow tone cast by some building or buildings on the opposite side of the street. Such a shadow tone may be shown with a definite upper edge, if this seems best, or it may be graded gradually into the white of the paper. In the former case it must be drawn correctly, or at least consistently, and at such an angle as not to introduce unpleasant lines.

Returning to the matter of making either the base or the top of a tall building the center of interest, we may add that a satisfactory composition when rendering a high structure of light material is to form a rather white area at its base, including within this area part of the building itself, the adjacent sidewalk, and possibly a portion of the street. This light area can often be made more conspicuous by adding contrasting darker structures adjoining the building shown. A dark street or shadow tone might also be added at the extreme bottom so the final composition would show a white area or spot surrounded by gray or black. This spot, punctuated by a few strong darks as in the doorway and lower windows, would provide a strong center of interest.

If the center of interest were for any reason wanted at the top, and the building was light in value, it might be advisable to leave the upper stories as a light mass against a dark sky, creating in that way a similar composition excepting for the shifting of the center of interest. Sometimes the opposite appearance would be more natural, however, gained by silhouetting the building rather darkly against a light sky or clouds.

It is points such as these which should be considered in doing the preliminary planning or sketching. Once a definite plan has been decided upon the rendering should be started and pushed forward according to it, the most common method being to render around the center of interest first, working out from there.

So far as technique is concerned there is no difference between the large structure and the small, with the occasional exception which is made when a heavier or coarser technique is used for the former. Such a technique is desirable if a drawing is large and is to be reproduced at rather small scale. If a drawing is made with no thought of reproduction, on the other hand, the technique must be fine enough to look well in the original.

Drawing from "Progressive Architecture"

INTERIORS AND THEIR ACCESSORIES

IN RECENT CHAPTERS we have discussed at length the representation of exteriors of buildings and their settings. Now we turn to a consideration of interiors and their accessories.

If one has had a fair amount of experience in the delineation of the former he should not find the latter particularly difficult. If, on the other hand, he has not drawn exteriors to any extent he will probably discover that it is necessary for him to do numerous preliminary exercises before attaining any real success in dealing with complete rooms. Many of these essential exercises would be in the practice of representing such building and finishing materials as are used for architectural portions of interiors, including stone, brick, plaster, tile, wood, and so on. One should also sketch the movable furnishings and furniture. If one has already done exteriors he will have had a fair amount of practice in this first direction, but he should join the novice in making studies of such items as have not entered into his other work, including particularly all sorts of upholstery materials, hangings, rugs, tapestries, and the like.

It is truly surprising what a variety of effects we find in these last things, so one should, as a preliminary to their attempted representation, learn to observe them intelligently. If one selects some fabric to draw, for instance, he should first study it carefully, looking at it close at hand and in the distance, in bright and in subdued light, laid out smoothly and in folds, searching always for its special characteristics under all sorts of conditions, and endeavoring also to retain mental impressions of these peculiarities for future use. Then he should compare one fabric with another, or drape several in such a way that they can be easily seen at one time. It is surprising what differences can be discovered even in plain materials by an inspection and analysis of this sort. A piece of satin and a piece of cotton cloth of similar color and tone will vary greatly, and even a light piece of cotton and a dark piece of the same material will show marked dissimilarity in effect, in addition to the contrast in value.

To make one or two suggestions: it will be noticed that light colored cloth usually shows more apparent contrast in its values than does darker material of a similar kind, as the dark color seems to absorb many of the lighter tones of shade and shadow. A smooth material with a sheen will not look at all like some dull fabric of similar tone, as it will have many highlights and reflections. Certain fabrics, such as velours, will sometimes appear dark where we expect to see them light, and light where other materials would be dark, and by rubbing the nap the effect can be changed instantly from light to dark or from dark to light. Many materials of a shiny nature grow dull and soft with age, but there are exceptions, for some others—leather for example—often become smooth and glossy with wear. The smoother the material the more complicated and changeable are its values, as a rule, and the stronger its highlights. Now when it comes to draped fabrics there is great difference in the way they hang, for some are hard and inflexible and others soft and yielding. Heavy materials usually hang quite straight and show fewer small folds and creases than do those which are light in weight. Heavy materials, too, are generally opaque, and for this reason are sometimes less difficult to represent than are thin nets and scrims and similar fabrics which are so translucent or even transparent as to show light, or occasionally objects, through them.

Perhaps we should not say so much concern-the representation of material before pointing out one of the really fundamental differences in the appearance of nearly all interiors and exteriors—a difference in the customary effects of light and shade. Exteriors, generally speaking, and particularly those of an architectural nature, are usually drawn under what we might call normal daylight conditions, in which case the sun is the sole source of direct illumination. The rays of the sun are considered, for this purpose, as being parallel; consequently the shadows cast are definite in shape and have a certain similarity of direction. The observing person can soon learn the shapes most commonly found and can apply them quite successfully when working from memory or the imagination. Direct sunlight, however, is largely excluded from interiors. What does come through the windows is often softened by curtains. There are exceptions, of course, in which areas of sunlight are formed as definite as those found outside. But if we consider interiors as a whole it is evident that the illumination is largely reflected; the light is therefore softened and diffused and the shadow shapes are variable and often indefinite. The shadows take many directions, the light generally radiating in a sense from each door and window; this brings about complexity of form and variety in edge and value. If the reader is now indoors, and it is daytime, let him observe for himself and he will probably find surprising differences in the value, direction, and character of the different visible shadow tones. Some edges are sharp and some so soft as to be almost lost. If a chair is placed within a few feet of a window but not actually in sunlight, and the shadows cast on the floor by the four legs are studied, certain interesting things may be noted. It will probably be seen that the shadows are radiating

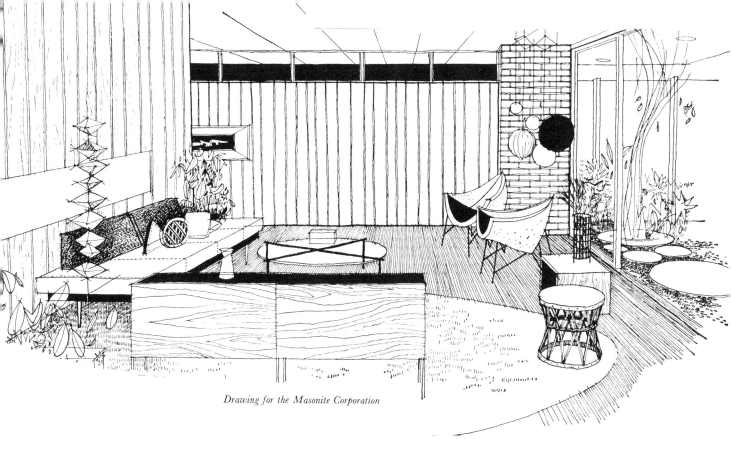

instead of parallel in direction, and that if each one is considered by itself it will reasonably dark and definite where the leg comes in contact with the floor but will grow light and indefinite and perhaps be lost as it spreads from this point of contact. If one touches the lead of his pencil to a sheet of paper, again he will note that the sharpest and darkest shadow appears nearest the point of contact.

This difference between the daytime shadows indoors and out is confusing in the sense that shadow shapes vary so indoors that it is not easy for one to become acquainted with them. Each source of light, such as each window, causes a new group of shadows, so that often in rooms where there are several windows the shadows cast by the light from each of these cross and re-cross in a highly disturbing manner. Much light within rooms is reflected upward from the brighter parts of the floor and furniture, giving

us some shadows in a direction almost opposite to that customary outdoors. The action of reflected light may be noted, for example, in the shadows of ceiling lighting fixtures. Though more varied, the main contrasts in interiors are seldom as sharp as in exteriors; there is greater effect of subdued lighting throughout. Contrarily there are perhaps more small accents of light and dark in interiors, which appear strong in relation to the other relatively subdued tones. These are caused mainly by the large number of smooth or polished surfaces which interiors offer to pick up light and reflect it. There are the shiny floors, for instance, and table tops, and doors, and polished pieces of furniture. Especially are there many brilliant small areas of highlight on such places as arms and backs of chairs, dishes, lighting fixtures and hardware.

Of course artificial illumination changes conditions both within and without. Generally speaking such light usually seems rather inadequate outdoors; consequently it is here that the softest effects are customarily seen at night. Interiors can be quite brilliantly illuminated with no great effort. This means that the night and day conditions in and out are practically reversed. As a rule, however, the shadows cast by brilliant artificial light indoors, though much like those cast by the sun outdoors so far as their definiteness is concerned, are caused by rays which, instead of being parallel, are radiating from the source of illumination. If there are several sources of artificial light—several different lights—again there may be a crossing and re-crossing of shadows to prove distracting. All this means that in drawing interiors, whether day or night, the student may be confused if he tries to understand and interpret every shadow —he must learn to simplify. It means also, however, that if he does make mistakes they may be less easily detected than similar mistakes on outdoor subjects in sunlight, so there are advantages and disadvantages in both. The important thing for the student to know is that there is this difference in general effect; knowing this he can do his own observing more intelligently.

There is another point of difference between most interior and exterior subjects which affects their handling. The man drawing exteriors, even if handicapped at times through being forced to draw more definite shadows, has, as compensation, great leeway in the use of accessories; if the sky seems empty he can add clouds; if the surroundings seem plain he can plant trees; if the architecture is bare he can make use of vines, flower boxes, etc. In a large percentage of interior work, contrarily, all of the architectural background is quite definitely fixed, and the artist has little opportunity to do more to aid his composition than arrange movable objects such as some of the smaller pieces of furniture,

though he sometimes does have recourse to potted plants.

While on this comparison of interiors and exteriors we should not fail to mention that ordinarily there is more variety in texture of material in the latter than the former, which sometimes gives opportunity for corresponding variety of technique.

There is still another common difference shown by many drawings of exteriors and interiors, and this is in the matter of perspective. For exteriors are usually viewed from a greater distance than interiors, thus making the perspective somewhat less angular and acute. Aside from this one fact, however, the perspective of both interiors and exteriors is more nearly the same than is sometimes realized. An interior is much like the inside of a box—an exterior like the outside of it. If this thought is kept in mind it may make the relationship between the two more apparent and helpful.

Drawing for the Masonite Corporation

Ordinarily the greatest difficulty in getting the perspective of interiors correct comes not in the handling of the architectural background, which so far as its general forms are concerned is usually quite simple, but in the placing and representation of the furniture. For to draw furniture well, correct in itself and at the same time right in relation to the rest of the room, is far from easy. In many drawings the individual pieces look too large or small or seem tipped up or wrongly foreshortened or incorrect in some way. For this reason, therefore, it is often best for the beginner to start his practice with the representation of single pieces of furniture. Fortunately there are always models available. Chairs are extremely good for first practice; as a rule they look their best if shown some distance away, so it is well to place each one across the room before sketching it. As for any type of subject, variety in selection should be sought, too.

The earnest student will doubtless like to try various methods, perhaps beginning with the more simple outline. He should not confine himself to furniture alone, however, but should

practice the representation of rugs, hangings, upholstery materials, etc. In all of these things he must learn to suggest or indicate pattern, as most such materials have more complex pattern than can be fully and accurately drawn in reasonable time and at small scale.

When one has learned to do these various details and portions of rooms to fair advantage he is qualified to attempt more comprehensive drawings of complete rooms or, more strictly speaking, of as much of each room as would customarily be viewed from one spot at one instant. Here again the method followed depends always on purpose or inclination.

During the last few years we have seen, particularly in the magazines, numerous drawings of interiors done in a combination of work in pen and wash. There are many effective treatments possible by this means. Sometimes when a pen drawing is not wholly successful a wash of some gray water color or diluted ink may be applied to it, or to parts of it, with helpful results. Often, however, the artist deliberately combines ink and wash, treating the entire draw-

Drawing for the Masonite Corporation

128

Vocational evaluation unit. Pennsylvania State University Press

ing, perhaps, in a somewhat sketchy way. Again, a more conventional combination of the two mediums is used. In most drawings of this type areas of solid black give the necessary accent. The possible combinations are almost limitless, the only necessary word of warning being a hint regarding the placing of these blacks, which must be arranged with the greatest care or they will destroy the balance of the composition or attract too much attention to non-essentials.

As a rule, in doing such work the objects to be represented are first outlined in ink, then the blacks are added with ink applied with either pen or brush, and finally the gray washes are "laid" in a few simple values. Often these washes are "flat" or graded in the simplest possible way.

The drawings so far described are all of the type used when the interior itself (or the furniture) is the center of interest or the actual subject of the sketch. Such drawings are most commonly employed by architects or decorators, or as illustrations for books or articles relating to home furnishing. Many are made, too, for advertising purposes. It should by no means be supposed, however, that this is the only sort of interior delineation which is done, for many times rooms or accessories such as furniture are used only as backgrounds or as settings for people. Here, as a rule, the opportunities are greater for suggestive interpretation; the artist must be extremely careful that these interiors or accessories do not become so important as to detract from his main thought.

We have now covered in a general way some of the most common kinds of interior drawings, though we recommend to the student here, as elsewhere, that he seek for many examples to supplement these which we have offered. For in this, as in every other field, there is no limit to the variety of treatments possible, to say nothing of the endless numbers and kinds of subjects available.

W, MORGAN

STUDYING WORK BY OTHER ARTISTS

THERE IS POSSIBLY NO WAY in which the student can learn more concerning pen drawing than through personal study of the best available originals or reproductions of work in that medium.

This statement needs defense, for there are those who might argue against it—who might claim that if a student honestly drew from real things without any recourse whatever to the results obtained by other artists, his drawings would have a vitality and interest not commonly gained. They might also claim that to study other drawings is merely to learn to mimic— that it stifles individuality, tending to force the artist into a rut from which he can extricate himself with difficulty, if at all.

There is something to this argument. Undeniably there is occasionally one who seems particularly gifted. Such a man, even though he had never seen a pen drawing, might work his own way through to the development of a satisfactory and original style of his own. If so, he would be a genius, and geniuses are rare. And even if he did this, it is also true that his drawings would of necessity still be much like those by other capable men, for the pen imposes the same technical limitations on us all.

We shall dismiss this method of always working directly from nature in one's own way, without reference to any examples of pen work, then, as not particularly suitable for the average student. He must regard the art of pen drawing as a growth, an accumulation to which each of many individuals has contributed his bit. To turn from or ignore the results of this accumulation would be for him pure folly.

Granting, then, that it is advisable for the student to study work by other artists, at least for a while, it is the purpose of this chapter to attempt to direct him along the analytical road which he must travel if he is to gain the greatest value from so doing.

First of all we should perhaps set him right on what may be termed a question of ethics. Is it wrong for one to copy a drawing, or parts of a drawing, done by some other artist, and then to take credit for the work, without making clear that it is a copy? Obviously the answer to this can be nothing but an emphatic affirmative. It would be as unfair for one to do this as it would be for him to copy word for word some literary creation, claiming the author's production as his own. There is no harm in the copying itself; often there is good. But the deliberate appropriation and giving out of the work of another as one's own is plagiarism, and conscious plagiarism is nothing short of stealing. If one copies work which he is to make public he should explain that his result is a copy, giving credit where it belongs. This doubtless seems perfectly clear. The beginner sometimes faces another question, however, which, though similar, has a less obvious answer. Has one the right to copy and use repeatedly the style of technique of some man whose work appeals to him? In other words how far can one honestly go towards "cribbing" technique, applying it to his own subjects? Generally speaking it is wrong to try to mimic another man's technique, particularly if he has an individual style which can be clearly identified as his own. There are men who have spent years in developing methods peculiar to themselves; to appropriate these wilfully in full would be nothing but dishonest. There are many little tricks of technique, on the other hand, which belong in no sense to any one individual; they are, instead, the common heritage of any or all

who wish to lay claim to them. A comparison of drawings will prove that there are enough of these to satisfy nearly every need of the student.

There is little danger, at any rate, that the student who works thinkingly will long be satisfied to mimic any one artist, for regardless of how clever that artist may be, it is seldom that all of his work will appeal in detail to any other artist. Even the student will soon find that he likes the way in which one artist suggests trees, but does not like his shadow tones, and so on. The beginner, then, in studying drawings for their technique, should compare many, seeking for what seems to him the most honest and satisfactory way of rendering each of numerous typical details.

Though technique is the first thing which the beginner is likely to study in the work of other men, he should not get the idea that it is all that can be learned from it. Nor is technique the most important thing in either their work or his own. One may become an expert technician and yet never be more than that; contrarily some artists whose technique in itself is far from being a commendable thing to study in detail have become famous for their work because of other fine qualities which it has. In fact it is often true that the artist who is strong in one direction is weak in another. The expert technician, for instance, may fail to select interesting or worth while subjects, or to compose them well when they have been selected. His work may also lack that rather intangible quality called "style." It is rarely that good technique is enough to overcome such handicaps as these.

Therefore one should learn to look beneath the technique for something deeper, striving to see the purpose the artist had in mind when he made his drawing. He should neither condemn a drawing too severely nor praise it too highly without thought as to how successfully the artist

Line drawing with tint block by EDY LEGRAND

132

Pen and brush drawing by HENRY RALEIGH

has carried out this purpose or intention.

In most published work this purpose of the artist seems quite evident; this leaves the student to decide to his own satisfaction whether or not it has been fulfilled. If one has selected for analysis a pen picture of an old house, for example, he should think about it in a way something like this: "Given this subject, has the artist made the most of it? Has he drawn it from the best point of view? Has he failed to include enough, or has he shown too much? What might have been omitted without detriment to the sketch? What might have been advantageously added or given more emphasis? Has he composed the whole well? Is the interest nicely centered on the house, or are there irrelevant or over-emphasized details to prove disturbing? Is the light coming from the angle which best expresses the subject? Does the house really look old? Would a more careless or free technique better express the age? Or should the expression of age be accomplished more through the drawing, perspective and the like, than through technique? Is the technique itself too conspicuous? What of the accessories; are they of the type and so handled as to contribute to the whole, or do they detract? Is the entire result convincing?"

Whatever the answers that one makes to his own questions—whether he is right or wrong in his conclusions as to the intended purpose of the artist or the success of the carrying out of that purpose—this whole process of analysis is sure to prove most helpful to the student. For if he analyzes in this way he will gain much more than he would by merely studying the technique. We emphasize this not because technique itself is unimportant, for it is not, but because the beginner often attaches too much importance to it. Of course a masterpiece of pen drawing should be technically excellent, but it must be much more than this. It must be of a worth while subject, if it is to have general appeal, and the subject must be brought out to the very best advantage in every way.

Now for a word about some of the common failings of the beginner which he can overcome if he honestly makes frequent comparisons between his own drawings and examples by the best artists. First of all, he too often fails to select interesting subjects. This does not mean that there is harm in doing commonplace things, such as we have shown in many parts of this volume, as aids along the line of progress. It does mean that in such drawings as one prepares for exhibition or publication he will usually be wise to try to present subjects which show beautiful or interesting things or which convey worth while messages of their own, or which supplement or illustrate some thought elsewhere expressed. Having made his selection the beginner frequently omits or suppresses important details which should be emphasized, and over-emphasizes non-essentials which should properly be omitted or suppressed. The result is lack of clarity and directness in the way in which the message is conveyed. He also fails, perhaps, to make of each drawing a good composition—a pleasing pattern or design. In fact, this particular quality of pattern is one of which most people are unaware unless it has been brought to their attention. Yet it is true that the silhouette or shape or pattern which a drawing makes against the paper surface is sometimes very interesting, and so adds to the pleasing effect of the whole. It is also true that the spotting of lights and darks within this silhouette needs real skill; the beginner too seldom thinks of this or has the ability to handle it. He perhaps fails to obtain proper balance or he gets two or more centers of interest of equal strength, so there is no dominant note in his composition. Possibly it is lacking in this good pattern or design quality in various other ways. Above all, however, the beginner's method is usually too indirect; he has not learned to use his means economically; he draws twenty lines where ten would do; he employs a dozen values where half that number would suffice; he covers large areas of paper surface, thus losing not only time and energy but also breadth and simplicity of effect, and he so over-emphasizes his technique that one is made too conscious of the lines themselves. The eager student will want to study the work of as many capable pen artists as possible. He should interest himself in specimens of work which he finds in books and magazines, cutting out and preserving such examples as especially appeal to him; there are many strong pen artists today from whose work one might advantageously make selections. He should try to collect as much material in this way as possible; it is not hard for the student to get, at almost no expense, reproductions worth many dollars to him if he learns to make full use of them.

As one gradually collects such material it should be filed in some systematic way and arranged according to different headings of interest. Drawings of landscape may be grouped together, for instance, and drawings of picturesque buildings such as old barns and mills. Other groups might contain illustrations of ships, people, animals and birds. It is valuable to group drawings according to types of technique, too. There are drawings done in pen alone, and drawings in pen and brush or pen and color or other such combinations of mediums. In fact the student can easily think of sufficient headings to serve all his purposes to advantage. Once the drawings are filed they should be taken out now and then, a few at a time, for analysis, comparison and enjoyment.

We must not close without mentioning that one should try to see and study original drawings whenever that is possible—they are more helpful in many ways than reproductions.

THE PEN COMBINED WITH OTHER MEDIUMS

UP TO NOW we have been concerned, almost entirely, with the more usual and orthodox performance of the pen. But it would be a mistake to have a restricted idea of its capabilities for the pen lends itself generously and naturally to manipulation with other mediums; or to be unaware that in ink drawing there is a kindred instrument of equal importance, the brush.

The brush is more nimble than the pen but for most it is more difficult to handle. It can move in any direction on the paper without any of the tripping hazards of the steel point. While all types of brush can be used with ink for special work, the only kind that has all-around firmness united with flexibility is the red sable. It should be of the best quality and numbers 3, 4 and 5 are the most usual sizes. They are expensive and should be treated with care—thoroughly washed after using, the points coaxed into shape and placed in a glass or container, points up, where their shape will not be disturbed.

The brush is obviously of great use in dealing with large areas of black which would be burdensome to cover with the pen, but the brush can be used like a pen too. In skillful hands it can produce lines as delicate as the most sensitive crow-quill point. In addition it can produce more variations of thickness in any given line than any pen. So the brush can be used in either a bold or sensitive way to make complete ink drawings or it can be used in happy conjunction with the pen.

HENRY C. PITZ
"Froissart's Chronicles"
Limited Editions Club

136

Dry brush

Split brush

The dry brush—The brush can produce two kinds of stroke which are impossible for the pen. The first is the drybrush stroke, a very simple operation. It does not work too successfully with small brushes, numbers 3 and up should be used. And a paper with some tooth to it gives the best results. The brush is charged with ink, then the greater part removed by a blotter or by brushing on scrap paper. Then, with the hairs of the brush spread fan-wise, the paper surface is stroked lightly. If properly done, lines with edges of interesting irregularity, and tones permeated with flecks of white paper, will be created. A good deal of practice and experimentation is necessary before accurate judgements of tone can be made.

The split brush—The split brush technique is akin to the dry brush. The lightly inked brush (an old, worn one is excellent) is splayed out on a bit of scrap paper so that the hairs separate into a number of points. These points can be arranged in any manner with a knife blade. A stroke from this brush will create a passage of multiple lines. It is an excellent method for quick cross-hatching and for rendering textures such as bark, grass, water and weathered wood. Both the above techniques unite well with the pen line.

Pen and wash—The pen line unites readily with many other mediums; one of the oldest combinations is pen and wash. If pen forms are drawn with waterproof ink, watercolor washes may be freely applied without harm to the basic

drawings. This is the oldest and most usual way, but a reverse method has come into increasing use. The major shapes and tones are washed in freely and directly and afterward defined and emphasized with a loose calligraphic ink line. Another method of increasing popularity is to draw directly with pen or brush into areas dampened with clear water. This method is difficult to control but can result in unpredictable and fascinating forms as the carbon in the ink deposits in strange swirls and patterns. On this and the following pages are examples of these methods.

Pen and Pencil—Most pen drawings are made over a skeleton sketch in pencil, but usually, and especially when the drawing is to be reproduced, the pencil lines are erased after inking. However, there are many times when a softening of the pen line or the introduction of tonal subtleties is desirable and no instrument is more convenient for this than the pencil. The many brands of graphite drawing pencils, with their range from very hard to very soft, are usually used. One type of drawing pencil, the carbon pencil, is particularly useful because it makes a velvety black line that blends well with the ink line and its mark is matt, without the shine of the graphite pencil. Another type, the lithographic pencil is particularly suited to supplement the pen drawing where reproduction by line plate is necessary. The lithographic pencil is a grease crayon that makes a rich, black mark; on textured paper it leaves flecks of black on the

Drawing for War Department by BARSE MILLER

innumerable little crests of the paper, making an interesting speckled tone. It also comes in stick form and many interesting effects can be obtained by using the edges sidewise.

Pen and charcoal—A seldom used, but effective and not difficult combination is charcoal over the pen line. It is a quick and easy way of imparting tonal body to a pen line drawing. The charcoal tones may be drawn in or rubbed in for subtle transitions and since charcoal is easily changed or removed, the artist can experiment freely with tonal distribution without harming the underlying pen drawing. The final rendering should be given a coating of fixatif.

Pen and Pastel—This is another seldom used combination. Pastel behaves in much the same way as charcoal, with the added advantage of color. It is a combination suitable for sketching. The color masses may be rubbed in rapidly and loosely, then thoroughly fixed and pen lines drawn over the color to define the forms.

The artist of today is much more eager to try new combinations of media than were his immediate ancestors. A great many lively and interesting effects have come out of such experimentation; this has removed many of the taboos about the "purity" of media that used to hamper the more adventurous artists.

WALTER KUMME
Scratch board drawing

SPECIAL MATERIALS AND ODD METHODS

THE PRESENT CHAPTER should be of especial value to the student of advertising drawing or illustration, though perhaps no less useful to the delineator of architecture.

Scratch board—Scratch board is simply a drawing board of fair weight having a white chalky surface. As a rule when one makes a drawing on it he covers with black ink all such areas as are finally to appear very dark, using a brush or broad pen. The brush is perhaps the better of the two for this purpose as the pen has a tendency to damage the surface by scratching. Black water color paint is sometimes substituted for the ink. When this black tone is thoroughly dry, white lines may be easily scratched through the black with a sharp knife.

In some drawings the entire surface is painted black, and all the light tones are obtained by scratching; as a rule this is a waste of time, however. In more instances the board, or at least a part of it, is drawn on with a pen or brush exactly like any drawing paper. The only difficulty in working on scratch board with the pen is that the sharp nibs have a tendency to scratch up and collect particles of the chalky surface, causing wide lines and blots. This difficulty turns some artists to the substitution of a fine brush for the pen; it is by no means impossible to do pen work upon it, however, if care is taken and if the points are frequently wiped.

Many tools may be used, etching needles, X-Acto knives, razor blade corners and dentist probes. One of the best is the triangular steel eraser or scratch knife. This is an inexpensive

Black ink or paint may be applied with a brush or large pen.

White lines may be scratched or engraved through the black ink with a knife.

White dots may be similarly scratched in the black.

Cross-hatch tones of white scratches are often most useful →

Scratch board effects

steel nib which fits into an ordinary pen holder. Good scratch boards are made in this country by the Charles J. Ross Company and Artone.

Special surfaces—Besides scratch board there are a considerable number of boards prepared with special surfaces for producing a variety of patterns when brushed with ink or the lithographic pencil. The Ross Company has a large number whose surfaces are pressed into minute dots, lines, grains and other forms. A lithographic crayon rubbed over the surface blackens the raised portions and reveals the pattern. If the surface is entirely painted over in black ink and then lightly scraped with a razor blade, the high spots in white reveal the pattern in reverse.

These white Ross boards are very popular, and drawings made on them reproduce very well. If not too much reduced such drawings are suitable for reproduction by zinc etching, even for newspaper work; much of the pencil drawing which appears in the newspapers, incidentally, is done on these or similar papers. If ink is used it may be scratched down to gray or to the pure white as shown in the samples.

It is fascinating to work on these papers; if they have any disadvantage it is that some of them prove rather trying to the eyes, and of course so far as pen work is concerned the roughness of surface prevents really excellent technique. One must work carefully, too, for once a surface is scratched away it cannot be restored.

Repro and Coquille boards are made by Grumbacher. These are white boards covered with special textures, such as various grades of stipple, beads and grains. These textures are revealed by the lithographic crayon or a Grumbacher Cartoonist pencil. These boards cannot be scraped or incised. They are usually used to simulate a halftone effect in a drawing that can be reproduced in line.

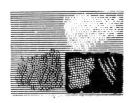

Various Ross-board patterns

Various textures made by rubbing lithographic crayon over thin paper placed over different surfaces such as linen, screening, leather, buckram

Printed and rubbed textures—A wide range of interesting effects can be created by pressing the textures of various materials onto a drawing. Leather, lace, wood, screens and many other materials may be brushed lightly with ink and pressed against the paper. Often a more satisfactory way is to glue the material to a block of wood and roll it lightly with a roller coated with prinking ink. Even one's inky fingers may make interesting patterns.

Rubbed textures may be created by placing tracing or bond paper over an interesting surface and rubbing with a lithographic pencil. Stone, wood, incised metal, book covers, plaster are just some of the surfaces that can give likely results.

Tricky methods—Occasionally one sees an original drawing which has much the appearance of scratch board work (and which would reproduce in the same way), yet close inspection, even with a magnifying glass, shows that such white lines as at first glance seem to be scratches really are not. An effect like this is often baffling to the uninitiated. It may be gained in any of the following ways.

A simple method is first to apply to the paper, with a pen or a fine brush, lines of a thick mixture of some opaque water color, such as Chinese white, exactly where it is intended that whites shall finally appear. When these lines are thoroughly dry waterproof drawing ink is washed over them and over such areas of the paper as are to be black when the drawing is finished. When this ink is dry, water is freely flowed across the entire drawing. This dissolves the opaque paint and removes it completely and along with it the ink with which it is covered. The rest of the ink, having soaked into the paper, is not injured, so the desired result is obtained.

In another method a heavy wax solution or a clear lacquer is applied for the whites, in the same way as the water color just mentioned, and the ink is then added. When dry, the proper solvent removes the ink-coated wax or lacquer without harm to the paper surface.

All this is getting away, to some extent, from conventional pen drawing, yet, as we have said, the pen artist, especially when seeking novel effects, usually like to be acquainted with many mediums and methods. Young artists, particularly, are attracted by unusual methods. Although they may be inclined to overdo the use of new techniques, in time they will learn to be more selective, to use unusual methods only when appropriate for the work being done.

HENRY C. PITZ
Book cover, Doubleday and Company

ILLUSTRATION IN PEN AND INK

PEN AND INK has been one of the most widely used illustrative mediums for many decades and still is. One of the reasons for its wide use is that it is a brilliant and clean-cut medium that imparts liveliness to the printed page and harmonizes with type forms. Another potent reason, a dollar and cents one, is that it can be reproduced by the cheapest of the usual reproductive processes.

Therefore, in illustration the ink drawing is almost always linked with the line-cut. And so many inventive uses have been worked out for line-cut reproduction, particularly in the use of colors *other than black*, that often the finished print is not recognized as the result of a series of ink drawings. One of the obligations of the illustrator or commercial artist is to familiarize himself with the techniques of printing, preferably by visits to printing establishments. There

are scores of little methods and tricks, made possible by a knowledge of printing methods, which enable the artist to get unusual and provocative effects by simple means and at modest cost. Technical ways and means are important in illustration.

The book field is a great user of line illustration, particularly the department of children's books. Children's books are almost always illustrated and a goodly proportion of the pictures are in black and white line. Also, a large proportion of the color pages are illustrated in flat colors, which are reproduced by line plates. Each of the colors used requires a separate drawing, called a color-separation, and these are often executed in ink.

A great many book-jackets—the decorated paper wrappers folded around the book covers—use line plates, usually in combinations of colors.

REINER ZIMNIK
Illustration from "Drummer of Dreams," Faber and Faber

Record-album covers are another rich field for the line-cut techniques and of recent years the paper-back book has spurred a whole school of designers.

Books of fiction are seldom illustrated but histories, biographies, travel books and reprints of the classics are frequently illustrated in line. Educational textbooks, particularly for the younger grades are using a large amount of illustrative material and this has become a rapidly expanding field that offers great opportunities to the young illustrator. There are always a certain number of special editions and illustrated gift-books that almost always gravitate to artists of reputation.

Pen and ink is not much used on the front pages of the large mass-magazines but a fair number of one- and two-color line spots may be found on many of the back pages among the departmental matter. Smaller magazines, trade journals, house organs, fraternal and organiza-tion periodicals often use a good deal of it and it predominates in most of the children's magazines and sunday school weeklies.

Advertising makes use of line in hundreds of ways, mostly in the smaller advertisements on periodical pages and in direct mail material—folders, booklets, cards, brochures, catalogs.

The newspapers need it greatly, to circumvent the hazards of cheap paper and rapid printing. Besides the advertising pages its use is wide spread in the cartoons, comic strips, sports sketches and special drawings and designs for the Sunday feature sections.

The field is large and the opportunities are excellent. A greater variety of technique and compositional approach is possible today than ever before. The new and provocative has more chance than ever. But it is not a field to be entered blindly; the artist needs special training or orientation.

The average art student is accustomed to

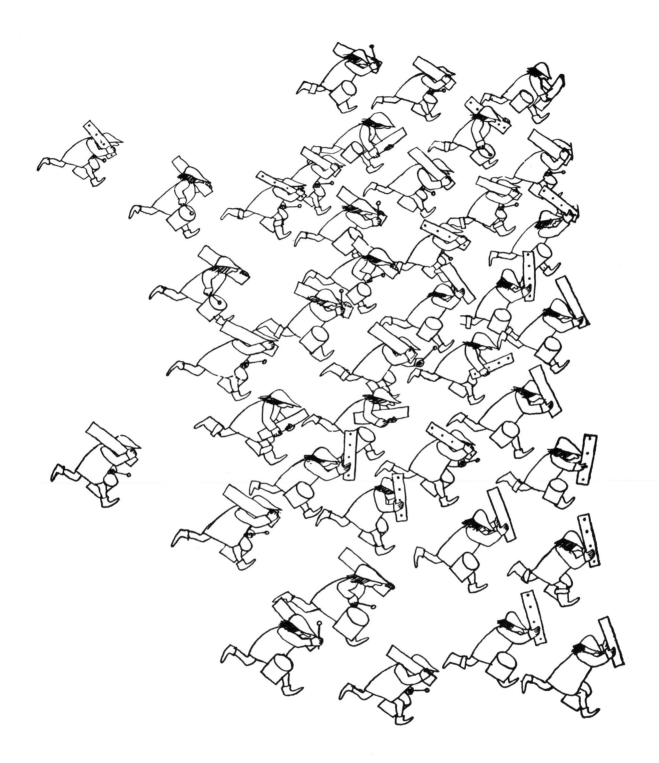

paint or draw according to whim. The illustrator must paint or draw to a definite purpose. He works for an editor or art director who represents a publication or an advertising agency—behind this is a public composed of thousands or millions of individuals. These individuals must have their attention captured. They will respond to a picture or design that touches their own experience. There must be communication.

The young artist will find his subject matter presented to him. Almost always he will be given a manuscript or some other kind of copy. He will have to study the text and absorb from it the material for his pictures—the characters, the setting, the mood, the action. This material he will try to glorify in pictorial terms but he dare not contradict the import of the text.

In addition there will be restrictions of size and shape; the pictures must conform to some type of reproduction and printing. Sometimes, as happens in most advertising commissions, the artist must follow the art director's layout.

It is an exacting profession and to prepare for it the young artist should be set many problems that will require him to work with definite texts, accurate dimensions and specific methods of reproduction. In short, the student's problems should be as much like actual assignments in the professional field as possible. The right kind of instructor will assign this kind of problem.

When the student feels that his efforts approximate professional standards, he is ready to cleanly mat or mount his best pictures, put them in a portfolio and make the rounds of the art director's offices. Unless he finds an agent, he must become his own salesman, visiting a series of publications or agencies from a list compiled from the yellow pages of the telephone books. This canvassing is not always easy for the young artist, but generations have done it and the art directors expect it. Art directors are often hurried but they are seldom unkind.

V. DOUGLAS SNOW

REPRODUCTION

SO VAST a subject is reproduction that we shall make no attempt to do more than offer a few brief hints and suggestions on such details of it as seem most essential to the pen artist. After all, the artist can best learn how to draw for reproduction through the experience of having his own drawings reproduced, for in this way he will profit from his mistakes. And even though it is important for one to have a general knowledge of the results obtainable by the various reproductive processes he really needs to know little of the processes themselves, unless, perhaps, he is a commercial or advertising artist who may be called upon to act in an advisory capacity concerning reproduction or printing. We shall assume here, therefore, that a superficial knowledge is sufficient, and so shall endeavor to avoid as far as possible long descriptions and confusing technical terms.

Practically all drawings at the present time, whether made in pen or some other medium, are reproduced by photo-mechanical processes, but the popularity of ink drawing for commercial uses is due partly to the fact that it can be reproduced by means of the line cut, the cheapest of the usual processes. In this process the black lines of an ink drawing are photographed on a sensitive film, the film transferred to a metal plate and after some manipulation is given an acid bath. The film protects the drawn lines and allows the acid to eat away the remaining metal. The drawing finally exists as a raised tracery in metal so that an inked roller passed over it

deposits ink only on the drawn image and ignores the lowered areas of metal. Now a sheet of paper pressed against the inked plate receives a replica of the inked image. Plastics and hardened rubber are now being used in addition to the traditional zinc and copper.

This is a very much condensed description of a rather intricate operation but it is not necessary for an artist to be aware of every minute detail. Visualization is difficult from a printed description, but a visit to a photo-engraving plant should be of great help.

The prints from a zinc etching come out solid black—or a solid color if colored ink is chosen—so the artist who draws for zinc etching usually makes his drawing of solid black ink or paint. Therefore graded effects may be obtained only through stippling with dots, through varied spacing of lines, or through the use of rough drawing papers which break up the lines or tones into irregular dots, lines, or other areas, each part of which will print black. There is also Ben Day work, later described.

Despite the fact that a zinc plate prints only in solid tone, black usually being chosen, we wish to make it clear that prints of any solid color may be made from the same plate, which is, in principle, exactly like a piece of type. This is simply a matter of having the printer use ink of the desired color, even though only a light tint is wanted. A point to remember is that every part of the plate which in printing comes in contact with the paper surface will print in the one solid tone of the ink used.

Another point is that zinc plates may be made not only from pure black drawings but from any original which has sufficiently dark photographic value. Reds, browns and oranges, for instance, photograph dark on the usual commercial negatives. Many light tints, however, particularly light blues, have no photographic value. Good black "copy" (as any subject submitted for printing is called) is the safest if fine results are required. White paper should always be used for drawings to be reproduced in line.

When the artist makes a pen drawing—or a brush drawing of like nature—for reproduction by line plate, he should be fully informed on a number of points, including the final size of the reproduction, paper to be used, quality of press work, etc. This first is very important, for one cannot hope to draw to the best advantage when he is unaware of at least the approximate size of the final reproduction. Many times the buyer of drawings, including even the trained advertising man, orders drawings without telling the artist the necessary reproduction sizes; the result is that the artist works under a distinct handicap. Some artists like to work at rather large scale and some at small. If a drawing is made large, however, without great reduction in mind, and then is reduced to any extent, the detail naturally becomes very fine. Not only does the effect seem finicky and overworked but some of the finer lines or dots may be etched away entirely or be left so weak that they will break down under a little use. With too much reduction, lines also often come so close together that the ink fills in the etched spaces between them, causing smudgy results. As a general thing, therefore, drawings should not be made too large, three times the final size being almost the maximum, unless, of course, an extremely simple and "open" technique is employed.

Sometimes drawings are even photographed up to a size larger than the originals. As a principle, however, the making of a plate larger than an original drawing or even at the same size should be condemned unless the drawing has been done with extreme care. It is not that there is any mechanical difficulty about doing this within reasonable limits, as it is simply a matter of changing the focus of the camera. The trouble lies mainly in the fact that any inaccuracy of drawing is emphasized in enlargement while at the same time a crudeness of technique often becomes evident. Reasonable reduction, on the contrary, makes such inaccuracies and technique less conspicuous.

The artist in working for reproduction must, of course, know how to make his drawings of the proper proportion to reduce to fill the required spaces. As a general thing one who has not had a great deal of experience will be wise to make a preliminary sketch at the exact size of the final, basing his larger drawing on it. The proportions of this sketch—or of the space itself if no sketch is made—may be enlarged in a number of ways. Often a scale is used; proportional dividers are also very commonly employed, being so accurate that some artists use nothing else. The pantagraph is used, too, but the cheaper ones are not sufficiently accurate for more than the general masses and larger details. In the drawing opposite we have illustrated several methods employing the diagonal, any one of which will serve the purpose.

In that at "1" we have assumed that the triangle *ABC* represents a small drawing to be enlarged, rectangle *abcd* indicating a margin line around it. If no such margin exists in a subject one should be drawn as an aid in construction. This, like the other construction lines, may be lightly drawn in pencil and later erased if desired.

One should next decide on the amount of enlargement needed. In our problem it was decided to make the final drawing half again as large as the original sketch, so line *bc* was continued to *c'*, *bc* being exactly two-thirds of *bc'*. The diagonal *bd* was also extended until it cut at *d'* a line drawn vertically from *c'*. From *d'* a horizontal was drawn back to *a'* located on a line extended vertically from *a*. We have therefore constructed rectangle *a'bc'd'* exactly similar to the original rectangle *abcd*, using the same diagonal produced.

From the points of the triangle *ABC* verticals have been drawn cutting line *ad* at *2, 1* and *3*,

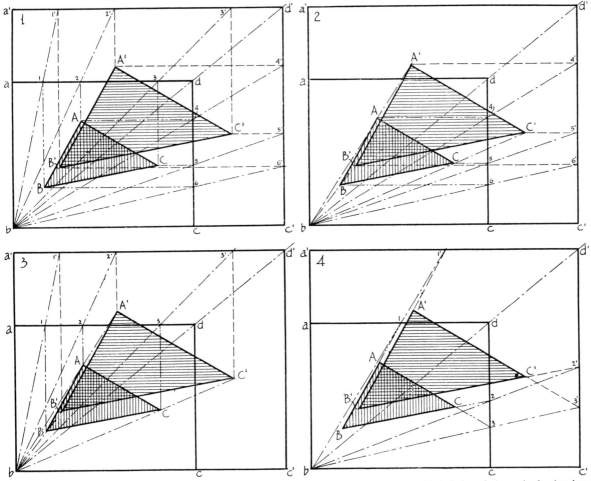

Methods for reducing and enlarging drawings

and horizontals cutting line *dc* at *4, 6* and *5.* Then with point *b* as a center, lines have been radiated through points *1, 2, 3, 4, 5,* and *6* cutting line *a'd'* at *1', 2'* and *3',* and line *d'c'* at points *4', 5'* and *6'.* Verticals have been dropped from points *1', 2'* and *3'* intersecting lines drawn horizontally through points *6', 4'* and *5',* respectively, at *B', A'* and *C'.* By connecting these latter points we have obtained the desired triangle *A' B' C',* exactly similar to *ABC* and half again as large, and located properly within its margin lines.

When the parts to be enlarged are not regular in shape like this triangle it is sometimes necessary to bound them with straight lines, enlarging the area so bounded. Curved line objects must be done in this way.

At "2" we have shown an easier method for subjects which are simple. This is much the

same as the method at "1," however, excepting that the vertical lines have been omitted from points *A, B* and *C.*

At "3" the verticals have been used but no horizontals. It is sometimes easier thus to refer the object to be enlarged to a horizontal edge of the bounding rectangle as here, and sometimes to a vertical edge as in the former method.

Method "1" is really a combination of "2" and "3" and hence more complex. It would be necessary only for complicated subjects.

Method "4" is somewhat different. In making the diagram the bounding rectangle itself was enlarged as before. Line *BA* was continued to cut *ad* at *1.* Lines *BC* and *AC* were also continued until they cut *dc* at *2* and *3.* Then from *b* as a center, lines were drawn radiating through points *1, 2* and *3* establishing *1', 2'* and *3'.* From these points lines were carried back parallel to

149

the sides of the original triangle, these lines meeting to form the required enlarged triangle $A'B'C'$.

Though line plates are often recommended even for rather rough or cheap papers, it is nevertheless true that nothing but a coarse and extremely open plate can be printed to advantage on anything but fairly smooth paper of good grade. One has but to look at newspaper stock through a magnifying glass, for example, to realize the folly of attempting to do any fine work upon it with any certainty of satisfaction. Fine detail naturally requires a smoother surface than coarse detail. If paper for printing is chosen before the artist starts his drawing he should be made acquainted with the fact and if it is rough or unusual in texture he should preferably be furnished with samples. Particularly for newspaper work the artist must make many allowances, for not only is the paper extremely cheap but the press work is very rapid and the ink poor. With the proper press work, surprisingly good results may often be obtained with cheap papers but it requires careful work; the best printing results can be gained only with excellent plates from drawings of the proper size printed with attentive supervision on good paper.

In much work for advertising where reproductions are to be made at several sizes, only one drawing is used. This frequently means that the smaller plates not only print with too much detail for their area but they may even fill in and smudge. For such purposes the artist should usually be commissioned to make at least two drawings of the one subject, the small one as the basis of the smaller reproductions being very simple.

Engraver's proofs—The only way in which one may be quite sure of the final effect is to have a plate actually made and proofs pulled on the stock to be used. Even then results may be deceptive for it is seldom that such proofs really show the true character of the finished printing. Usually after a plate is made a proof is submitted by the engraver which is supposed to show how the plate will print. These engraver's proofs are often very deceptive, for in making them the engraver uses an especially prepared

paper, as a rule, which is so highly coated as to present an exceedingly smooth and perfect surface. And he pulls his proofs patiently, using an excellent ink; naturally the result is quite different from the best final prints which one can hope for in the work of the fast-running presses. Especially is this true for work which goes on rough paper or cheap newsprint stock.

If one demands particularly good plates he should go to a reliable house and explain the special work that is required. In this case he should look over these engraver's proofs with the greatest care, not allowing himself to be misled by them. He should study them inch by inch, comparing them with the original drawings. If they are not reasonably satisfactory the plates should be refused or changes should be demanded in them. This is assuming, naturally, that one is expecting to pay a price consistent with the best available work. If plates are found to be under-etched or over-etched, or with routing carelessly done, or essential lines or dots etched or routed away, or with scratches on them, they should be refused. Sometimes one cannot tell whether the work is good or bad in all respects unless he examines the plates themselves.

Patching drawings—It is far cheaper and better on the whole for the artist to make sure that each drawing is exactly right before a plate is made of it than to depend on hand tooling or changes on the plate itself, unless he is deliberately depending on the engraver to do something which is recognized as a natural part of his legitimate work. If an original drawing is made solely for the purpose of reproduction, so that its appearance does not especially matter, lines which are drawn and then found unnecessary may be painted out with white. Or patches of paper may be pasted over any parts which are not wanted or which need to be redrawn, any new work being done directly on the patches. If the original is to be used for other purposes in addition to reproduction it may be necessary for one to do the patching very carefully. It is often possible, in fact, to patch a drawing so that the work is scarcely visible, though to do this of course takes care. For such results the paper

WILLIAM E. HEITLAND

used for the patch should match that on which it is to be used. Often the patch can also follow exactly some pen line so that its edges will coincide with the line itself. If the paper is thick the patch may be turned over before it is pasted and the edges rubbed down with very fine sandpaper until extremely thin. Then the patch may be pasted or glued in place. If glue or paste runs out from beneath the patch it should be wiped or washed off if any line work is to be done there, as it is difficult to draw over even a thin coating of most such adhesives. As the dampness of paste or glue sometimes warps the paper a bit, many artists prefer to avoid this by using rubber cement. Mounting tissue such as is employed for mounting photographs is excellent, too, and is constantly gaining in favor. It is obtainable in almost any photographer's supply store either in small packages or large sheets, and should be applied according to the manufacturer's simple directions. Patches should be as thin as possible lest they cast a shadow which will reproduce like a drawn line.

Special plates—The artists are indebted to the engravers for many things, for they are able to do a great deal which saves the time and trouble of the artist. If, for example, a border is to be carried around a page, repeating a certain motive, it is possible for the engraver to make up a complete plate of this border from a drawing of a single motive. Or if a design is to be repeated in a reversed position, as on the opposite side of a page, this may be done. In the case of a bisymmetric design a plate of the whole can be made from a drawing of one-half. Or an entire subject may be reversed in value, the blacks appearing white and the whites black. If a plate is made in which the subject is shown reversed in direction from the original it must be checked with care to make sure that lettering is not running backwards, or that traffic is not on the wrong side of the street, etc. In case any such unusual plates are wanted, brief but definite instructions to the engraver should be written on each drawing.

Ben Day work—Among the things which the

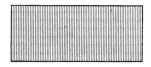

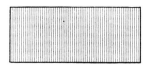

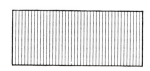

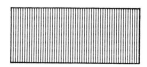

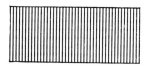

Ben Day tints

engraver can do to save the time of the artist who draws for reproduction we should not fail to mention the possibilities of the Ben Day Process. For by the use of certain labor-saving devices invented by Benjamin Day and now controlled by Ben Day, Inc., it is possible for the engraver to add to any portion of the reproduction of an artist's drawing, any of a large number of stipples, linings, and patterns. This is done by mechanical means which we shall shortly explain. In our margins we show samples of typical Ben Day screens but these are only a few from over a hundred which are available, to say nothing of many practical combinations. The artist who expects to make much use of this process should have at hand a book of proof sheets of the Ben Day "rapid shading mediums," as they are called by the manufacturer. These Ben Day mediums or "screens" themselves are really nothing but semi-transparent films, each mounted on a frame of wood. Each has dots or lines or patterns in relief on one side of it, corresponding to the printed samples in the book. These screens are inked by roller and printed on the metal plate, the negative, or even on the original drawing, by pressure on the back. Usually this printing is done on the metal plate with a special ink which is sticky; next the plate is dusted with powder much as we have mentioned in connection with the making of zinc etchings. This powder, when heated, melts and forms an acid resist so that when the plate is etched in the acid bath the Ben Day pattern is left in relief and so will print on paper like any relief matter.

Naturally it is seldom that a single Ben Day tint would be wanted all over a plate; usually it is confined to certain definite areas. The artist's drawing is generally photographed and printed photographically on the metal exactly as though it were to be etched as a regular line cut. Before the etching is done, however, the Ben Day tints are laid. In order to prevent a Ben Day film from printing its pattern all over the face of the plate it is necessary to confine it to the desired area by "stopping out" or "gumming out" all the rest. This is accomplished by painting the parts of the plate not to be

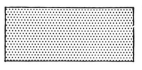

Ben Day tints

treated by the Ben Day with gamboge, a water color pigment. This must of course be so carefully applied that it comes exactly to the edges where the Ben Day film is to start, bare metal being therefore left where the film is to come in contact with the surface of the plate. It is at this time that the film is inked and applied to the plate as described above, printing its pattern on the metal. When the metal plate is next washed with water the ink resists the water and so is not washed off, but the gamboge washes away taking with it whatever ink may have printed onto it. Then the dusting or "topping up" is done, the plate is heated to make it acid resisting and is then ready either for etching or for the laying of the next Ben Day tint.

We have mentioned that it is not only possible to apply Ben Day to metal plates in this way but that they may also be laid directly on the negative; tints laid on negatives become reversed when on the metal, black on white becomes white on black, etc. The tints may also be applied to original drawings; naturally if used on drawings intended for reduction the Ben Day tint will reduce in size in proportion to the rest, a matter for which due allowance must be made.

These are only a few of the uses of Ben Day, but are perhaps the most valuable ones for the pen artist. The artist often works in outline, or outline combined with areas of black, next selecting the tints which he wishes the engraver to lay in different places. Inasmuch as blue wash or pencil has no photographic value the artist often blue-pencils such areas as are to be done in Ben Day, noting also the number of the film or films to be employed. Sometimes Ben Day work is done without any boundary lines around the tints, in which case a blue wash or a blue pencil outline is carefully applied to show the limits of the desired tone.

Shading Sheets—To an increasing degree, Ben Day effects are being incorporated by the artist directly on his drawings. He does this by using transparent sheets on which are imprinted various patterns of dots, lines, grained textures and other tones. Craftint and Zip-A-Tone are two well known brands of this type of film. They offer a wide variety of patterns and tones. The proper one is selected by the artist, laid over his drawing and cut to the desired shape with light pressure on a razor blade. Then the film is fastened in place by pressure so that the adhesive on the back takes hold, or by scotch-tape or rubber cement. By using two or more films, one over another, and changing the angles of the patterns, a great variety of effects are possible. If the artist takes the trouble to use these films he not only sees before him exactly how his drawing will reproduce, but he will be saving his client a certain proportion of the engraving costs.

The field for pen drawing—The field for the pen illustrator is large. A great deal of book illustration, particularly for children's books is done in ink technique, often with a second, third or fourth color added. The separations (individual drawings for each color) are also usually executed in ink. Line drawings are widely used in certain types of advertising, particularly for cards, booklets, catalogs, folders, fillers and all kinds of direct mail advertising. It is not used very much in the large, mass magazines but appears extensively in the smaller magazines and trade journals. It is widely used in newspapers, not only on the advertising pages but in the comic strips, cartoons and sports drawings. The economy of the line cut is still a big factor in the popularity of ink drawings.

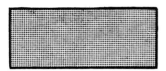 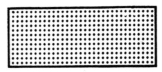 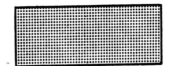

Sample Zip-A-Tone shading films

BEYOND TECHNIQUE

ALMOST EVERYTHING that has been said in the preceding chapters has revolved around matters of technique. That is the purpose of this book. But it would be a pity to leave in any reader's mind the impression that technique is the beginning and end of picture making.

Technique is a means to an end, a weapon, a servant, a necessary discipline, an enormous creative asset, if mastered. Once competence has been acquired, technique becomes largely a sub-

conscious function. It operates unawares as the mind knits itself other and more important problems. It becomes a source of confidence as the artist finds himself capable of solving more and more pictorial difficulties, as he cuts down the percentage of failures, as he experiences, at least occasionally, the taste of success.

With the satisfaction of a reliable technique at command, the artist is free to search his mind and heart for the things that he wants to put into

CAESAR
DIVIAVG·
DOMITIA
IMP·VI

ARÆTV
VALEA

JOSEPH CLEMENT COLL

his pictures. He will search not merely for subjects but for moods, sensations, insights—the things he knows and loves, the things that ignite his imagination. They can be big or little things, they can be anything, but they must be his own. This may sound easy and commonplace but it is difficult and a thing of wonder. It is a program for a lifetime.

After all, the true artist makes a lifetime commitment. His early efforts may be grueling and discouraging, but he should remember that discouragement feeds on itself. Everything favors the man who persistently picks up his pen and brushes in spite of doubt and hesitation. He should count himself lucky that he can spend his years in one of the provinces of the imagination, seeing more and dreaming more than most. It is a climate for thriving and growing.

To feed the process of growth, the young artist should enlarge his outlook by doing certain practical things. He should keep alert to current exhibitions, should try to dissect and get at the roots of the pictures that interest him, should mentally hang his pictures beside the others and try to make just comparisons. He should submit his pictures to juries and try to place them where they might find an audience. He should comb the art magazines and become familiar with the books in his field, past and present. If he is an illustrator or commercial designer he should keep in touch with current work, clip it if possible and file it away. He should pin on the walls of his studio the things that he admires and which might goad him into doing his best. He will find, perhaps, a number of clubs or organizations to bring him in touch with artists he would like to know. He may find that a day or evening class in painting or drawing might give his spirits a lift.

But the best school is life itself. If the artist can keep his mind and his eyes sharp, he will have no scarcity of material or lack of purpose. His subject matter is everywhere around him— he is surrounded by nature, by people and the work of people. All this is free for the taking and the taking is limited only by one's competence. So we come back to technique, for technique is *competence of doing*. Add to this *competence of seeing* and *competence of planning* and the result will be successful pictures.

RONALD SEARLE
Copyright: "Holiday" Magazine

A List of Selected Books

Byrnes, Eugene, editor, and Bishop, A. Thornton A COMPLETE GUIDE TO DRAWING, ILLUSTRATION, CARTOONING AND PAINTING, Simon and Schuster, New York, 1947.
An ambitious anthology of separate articles, some devoted to the ink techniques.

Cutler, Meritt HOW TO CUT DRAWINGS ON SCRATCHBOARD, Watson-Guptill Publications, New York, 1960.
A valuable book on scratchboard technique.

Fawcett, Robert ON THE ART OF DRAWING, Watson-Guptill Publications, New York, 1958.
A definitive book on drawing.

Guptill, Arthur L. PENCIL DRAWING, STEP BY STEP, Reinhold Publishing Corporation, New York, 1949.
Although it does not deal with ink techniques, there are many chapters on landscape, trees, water and other forms of nature.

Higgins Ink Company TECHNIQUES, Brooklyn, N. Y.
An inexpensive 48-page booklet.

Hoar, Frank PEN AND INK DRAWING, The Studio Publications, London and New York, 1955.
A good English publication.

Pitz, Henry C. DRAWING TREES, Watson-Guptill Publications, New York, 1956.
Devoted to the specialized subject of trees. Many techniques, including pen, brush and ink discussed.

Pitz, Henry C. INK DRAWING TECHNIQUES, Watson-Guptill Publications, New York, 1957.
Covers all ink techniques. Richly illustrated.

Pitz, Henry C. SKETCHING WITH THE FELT-TIP PEN, The Studio Publications, Inc., New York and London, 1959.
A manual on the newest ink tool, the fountain brush or felt-tip pen.

Watson, Ernest W. COMPOSITION IN LANDSCAPE AND STILL LIFE, Watson-Guptill Publications, New York, 1959.
A fresh and valuable insight on the structure of pictures.

Out of Print But Worthwhile Searching For

Bradshaw, Percy V. THE MAGIC OF LINE, The Studio Publications, London and New York, 1949.
Filled with reproductions of line drawing (including many ink techniques) from the present day back to the cave dweller.

Cole, Rex Vicat THE ARTISTIC ANATOMY OF TREES, J. B. Lippincott Co., Philadelphia, 1915.
A most comprehensive survey of the artist's approach to trees.

Garratt, Geoffrey LANDSCAPE DRAWING IN PEN AND INK, Pitman Publishing Corporation, London and New York, 1950.
A useful British manual.

Havinden, Ashley E. LINE DRAWING FOR REPRODUCTION, The Studio Publications, New York and London, 1938.
A manual of line illustration written from the British point of view.

Laver, James ADVENTURES IN MONOCHROME, The Studio Publications, London and New York, 1941.
A stimulating picture book, including ink techniques, with brief text.

Maginnis, Charles D. PEN DRAWING, Bates and Guild Co., Boston, 1921.
A small, early manual but still excellent for the student of today.

Maxwell, Donald SKETCHING IN PEN AND INK, Pitman Publishing Corporation, London, 1936.
A chatty book on drawing the English scene.

Pennell, Joseph PEN DRAWING AND PEN DRAUGHTSMEN, The Macmillan Co., New York, and T. Fisher Unwin, Ltd., London, 1920.
A landmark in pen and ink literature. A revised edition of an earlier work.

Pitz, Henry C. PEN, BRUSH AND INK, Watson-Guptill Publications, New York, 1949.
All the ink techniques in relation to landscape, the figure and illustration.

Simon, Howard 500 YEARS OF ART IN ILLUSTRATION, World Publishing Company, New York, 1945.
Over 450 pages of illustration, mostly in line of famous talents of all time, with commentary.